Henry E. Shepherd

The History of the English Language

from the Teutonic Invasion of Britain to the Close of the Georgian Era

Henry E. Shepherd

The History of the English Language
from the Teutonic Invasion of Britain to the Close of the Georgian Era

ISBN/EAN: 9783337086800

Printed in Europe, USA, Canada, Australia, Japan

Cover: Foto ©ninafisch / pixelio.de

More available books at **www.hansebooks.com**

The History

of the

English Language

from the

Teutonic Invasion of Britain

to the

Close of the Georgian Era.

BY

HENRY E. SHEPHERD,

Professor of the English Language and English Literature,
Baltimore~~ City College.~~

NEW YORK:
E. J. HALE & SON, PUBLISHERS,
Murray Street.
1874.

PREFACE.

This work is a History of the English Language, not a history of English Literature. Its design is to trace the growth and formation of our tongue, the influences that have affected its development, or have impressed upon it certain characteristics. All purely literary criticism is therefore irrelevant, except so far as it may tend to illustrate the peculiarities of the language, or to explain its apparent anomalies and its complexities. The book contains the substance of the Lectures delivered to the advanced classes in English in the Baltimore City College during the past three years, and is intended for the purposes of instruction in Colleges, High Schools, and Academies, as well as to meet the wants of general readers. The necessity for some work similar in design to the present must be obvious to all teachers of the English language in the United States. The want of suitable text-books constitutes one of the most serious obstacles with which the magnificent and rapidly expanding science of English Philology has to contend upon this side of the Atlantic.

It is but just to acknowledge in grateful terms the assistance derived from many excellent treatises, English, German, French, and American. Especial acknowledgment is due to the admirable publications of the Early English Text Society, and the Clarendon Press Series. With these remarks, the work is submitted to the consideration of teachers and of all persons desirous of promoting the scientific study of the English Language in the United States.

CONTENTS.

INTRODUCTION.

	PAGE
THE ARYAN OR INDO-EUROPEAN LANGUAGES	9

CHAPTER I.
ANGLO-SAXON PERIOD. A. D. 449–A. D. 1066 ... 19

CHAPTER II.
THE NORMAN CONQUEST ... 32

CHAPTER III.
THE INFLUENCE OF THE NORMAN CONQUEST UPON THE ANGLO-SAXON TONGUE ... 40

CHAPTER IV.
TRANSITION OF SAXON INTO ENGLISH ... 49

CHAPTER V.
THE WORKS OF THE TRANSITION PERIOD ... 55

CHAPTER VI.
THE RISE OF THE ENGLISH LANGUAGE ... 63

CHAPTER VII.
THE RISE OF THE ENGLISH LANGUAGE—*(continued)* ... 72

CHAPTER VIII.
PIERS, THE PLOWMAN ... 78

CHAPTER IX.
THE WYCLIFFITE VERSIONS OF THE SCRIPTURES ... 84

CONTENTS.

CHAPTER X.
THE ENGLISH LANGUAGE IN THE AGE OF CHAUCER.......... 89

CHAPTER XI.
THE AGE OF CHAUCER AND GOWER......................... 94

CHAPTER XII.
THE AGE OF CHAUCER AND GOWER—(*continued*)............. 98

CHAPTER XIII.
THE PRONUNCIATION OF THE ENGLISH LANGUAGE IN THE AGE OF CHAUCER.. 106

CHAPTER XIV.
THE VOCABULARY OF THE ENGLISH LANGUAGE............. 112

CHAPTER XV.
THE VOCABULARY OF THE ENGLISH LANGUAGE—(*continued*).. 128

CHAPTER XVI.
THE ENGLISH LANGUAGE FROM CHAUCER TO CAXTON. A. D. 1400–1474... 140

CHAPTER XVII.
THE INFLUENCE OF PRINTING UPON THE ENGLISH LANGUAGE. 143

CHAPTER XVIII.
THE ENGLISH LANGUAGE FROM THE COMMENCEMENT OF THE SIXTEENTH CENTURY TO THE ACCESSION OF ELIZABETH. 1500–1558... 148

CHAPTER XIX.
THE FORMATION OF ELIZABETHAN ENGLISH................ 155

CHAPTER XX.
ELIZABETHAN ENGLISH................................... 165

CHAPTER XXI.
THE ELIZABETHAN ERA. 1580–1625...................... 173

CHAPTER XXII.

THE TRANSLATION OF THE SCRIPTURES................... 181

CHAPTER XXIII.

THE CHANGES IN THE ENGLISH LANGUAGE SINCE THE ELIZABETHAN ERA... 185

CHAPTER XXIV.

THE ENGLISH LANGUAGE FROM THE CLOSE OF THE ELIZABETHAN ERA TO THE RESTORATION, 1625–1660............ 190

CHAPTER XXV.

THE ENGLISH LANGUAGE DURING THE RESTORATION. 1660–1685.. 195

CHAPTER XXVI.

THE ENGLISH LANGUAGE FROM THE CLOSE OF THE ERA OF THE RESTORATION TO THE ACCESSION OF QUEEN ANNE, 1685–1702.. 202

CHAPTER XXVII.

THE ENGLISH LANGUAGE FROM THE ACCESSION OF QUEEN ANNE TO THE DEATH OF DR. JOHNSON. 1702–1784....... 213

CHAPTER XXVIII.

THE ENGLISH LANGUAGE FROM THE DEATH OF DR. SAMUEL JOHNSON (1784) TO THE CLOSE OF THE GEORGIAN ERA (1830).. 222

INTRODUCTION.

THE ARYAN OR INDO-EUROPEAN LANGUAGES.

The languages of the Aryan* or Indo-European family may be divided into the following classes: The Sanskrit and its dialects, the Persian or Iranic, the Greek, the Latin, the Gothic or Teutonic, the Sclavonic, the Lithuanian, and the Celtic. The former of these designations is a term of comparatively recent introduction into the science of language, and is probably derived from the primitive home of the race, Arya, the central highlands of Asia. The word, according to some etymologists, is related to the Latin root *ar*, to plough (*arare*), old English *ear:* Piers Ploughman's Vision; Genesis, 45th chap.; Shakspere, Richard II.; and is indicative of the agricul-

---

* Judging from the evidence of language, the Aryan tribes seem to have made considerable progress in civilization before their migration from their original home. The words pertaining to peaceful occupations are the same in most of the dialects of this family, while those relating to the chase and to warlike employments are different. Terms in familiar use, some of which indicate a condition of society decidedly advanced beyond mere barbarism, are the same in most languages of this class. Such, for example, are the words for *king, door, plough, daughter, mother, father, son, sister, father-in-law, son-in-law, mother-in-law, daughter-in-law, brother-in-law*, the words for clothing, weaving, sewing, and the numeral systems from ten to a hundred.

tural habits of those to whom it was applied. The term Aryan does not appear to have met with general acceptance, and it is perhaps liable to objection, as its application is restricted almost entirely to one branch of the linguistic family, the Persian, and does not assign to the others their proper degree of importance. The latter designation (Indo-European) is intended to point out the territorial position and the geographical connection of the races which speak the languages it represents. There have been various attempts made to assign some definite locality as the original home of the Indo-European or Aryan family. Such efforts, however, have resulted in ingenious speculations, and we have not even a plausible tradition which will assist us in forming a determinate and satisfactory conclusion. There can exist no reasonable doubt, however, that, at a period antecedent to authentic history, the Indo-European race constituted one community or society; associated by the natural and easy ties of a common language and a common faith. We are not in this regard so destitute of evidence, for the absence of historic testimony is to a considerable degree compensated by the proofs of linguistic relationship, which all the dialects of this widely extended family present. In some instances the resemblance is clear and well defined ; in others the lineaments are marred, and almost effaced ; but whenever subjected to the rigid test of scientific comparison, the blurred outlines reveal their primitive identity and ancient kinship.

Let us now examine in detail the dialectic divisions of the Indo-European languages. At a period anterior to the rise of history, the different tribes began their migrations towards the West. It is commonly assumed that the Celtic migrations preceded the others, but this hypothesis rests upon no more substantial basis than the confused and inconsistent legends transmitted to us by these tribes. From the earliest times, Germany is inhabited by the Germans. This much at least seems probable, that the Sclavonic was the last branch that wandered far to the West. The Sclavonians retain nearly the same area which they at first occupied, and it is within a comparatively recent period that they have begun to acquire the elements of civilization. Of the different classes into which the Indo-European or Aryan family is divided, the Gothic or Teutonic class possesses for the student of the English language an immediate value, and demands careful investigation. Its dialectic divisions are: First, The Germanic, which is again divided into the Mœso-Gothic, the Old Saxon, the Low German, the Dutch, including the Flemish, the Frisic, and the High German. Second. The Scandinavian branch, which comprehends the Icelandic, the Swedish, the Danish, and their parent, the old Norse.

The Mœso-Gothic (Gothic of Mœsia) is the oldest representative of this branch. Early in the fourth century, one division of the great Gothic family settled in Mœsia, became subject to the Roman government, and was converted to Christianity. Ulfilas, their famous bishop, who was identified with the sect of Arius, translated the Scriptures into Gothic for the benefit of his countrymen, a design displaying remarkable boldness and power, as the influence of the classic languages was then predominant, and no others were deemed worthy or capable of literary culture. The Low German comprehends many dialects in common use in the low country, or northern parts of Germany. The Frisic occupied nearly the same territorial area with the Old Saxon, the coasts and islands of the North Sea. The Frisic exhibits a marked resemblance to the English. The Dutch has been spoken in Holland since the thirteenth century, although its literary pre-eminence dates from the sixteenth. The Flemish, in the thirteenth century, was the speech of the court of Flanders, and has its own records; it is now almost entirely supplanted by the Dutch. The Old Saxon was the principal dialect of Northern Germany, between the Rhine and the Elbe. It is preserved to us in the Heliand, or Saviour, a work which must be referred to the ninth century. The term Old Saxon is used to distinguish the language of the Continental tribes from that spoken by the Teutonic invaders of Britain, after their conquest of that country. There is no Continental language to which Anglo-Saxon can be affiliated. It accords most nearly with the Frisic. But it is most probable that it was indigenous in England, being formed by the gradual blending of the many Teutonic dialects introduced by the various Germanic invaders, the British tribes, and the Romanized inhabitants who spoke the Lingua Rustica Romana, in various corruptions. The High German is the language of learning and literature in Germany, and has been so since the reign of Charlemagne. Its complete ascendency, however, dates from the Reformation, and the translation of the Bible by Luther.

At the beginning of the great religious revolution in the sixteenth century, there prevailed in Germany the same discordance and variety of dialects which existed at the era of the Saxon conquest of England. Since the introduction of Christianity, several of the Germanic idioms had asserted their claims to literary pre-eminence. The Alemannic, Frankish, and Bavarian tongues had each become the medium of literary effort; then the Swabian dialect acquired the superiority, and it still contains some of the most cherished memorials of German heroism. The language of Luther, acquiring an intensified force from the invention of printing, and the impulse communicated to theological investigation by the revival of classical literature, permeated every part of the country, and became the general medium of all grades of society. This language was not the idiom of any district or any class, but one which had already established a just claim to be regarded as a literary speech, since it constituted the official language of the most important principalities in Southern and Central Germany. It was universally acknowledged as the language of literature and learning, and since that period its ascendency has been undisputed. Whatever dialectic peculiarities may exist among the uneducated, those who control the intellectual forces of Germany, those who compose the refined and educated classes, speak and write nothing else.

The High German may be divided into three epochs; the present or New High German, which dates from the time of Luther; the Middle High German, extending back from Luther to the twelfth century ; the Old High German, extending back to the ninth century.

The earliest literary memorials of the Scandinavian branch come to us from Iceland, where Christianity exercised a more conservative influence than in Germany, and did not destroy the ancient historic and religious movements. These are the two Eddas, which are both valuable on account of their antiquity, being the oldest productions of Norse literature, as well as on account of the information they convey respecting the primitive condition of the Germanic race. The Icelandic preserves most closely the primitive Scandinavian type. The Norwegian, the Danish, and the Swedish, are cultivated languages, the Norwegian bearing the nearest relationship to the ancient Norse tongue. The others are descended from more ancient dialectic divisions of Scandinavian speech.

The Celtic branch consists of two divisions: First, the Gaelic, comprehending the primitive language of Ireland, the language of the Scottish Highlanders,* and the Manx of the Isle of Man. Second, the Cymric, the speech of

---

* The Scottish dialect (Lowland Scotch) spoken in the southern parts of Scotland, is entitled to a recognition in our classification of languages. This is an Anglo-Danish dialect, formed chiefly by the admixture of Anglian or Germanic elements (the Angles, in their original occupation of Britain, having spread extensively over the Lowlands of Scotland, as the Danes did afterwards), and Danish or Scandinavian forms, and containing very few Celtic words. After the conquest of England by the Normans, many of the expatriated Saxons took refuge in Scotland, and thus considerably increased the Germanic population that had already been established between the Tweed and the Forth. The kings of Scotland received these exiles with especial distinction, and promoted them to positions of dignity and honour. The same generous hospitality was accorded to men of Norman race, who were dissatisfied with their share in the distribution of the spoils, or who had been expelled from England by the decree of the conqueror. These banished or discontented Normans resorted to the court of Scotland, where they were received into service, and invested with important military commands. The Scottish monarchs, in order to render their court more attractive to their Norman guests, endeavoured to engraft upon the Teutonic dialect already spoken there, many French terms, and French constructions. These foreign idioms were gradually naturalized in the region south of the Forth, and the national language of that part of the country soon became an equal admixture of Germanic, Scandinavian, and Norman French. The Scottish dialect is rapidly hastening to decay; before the end of the present century it will probably be confined to the humble and uneducated classes. A hundred years ago it was current among the higher ranks of society, and at the beginning of the present century it was intelligible to every one. Its literary ascendency was destroyed at the Reformation, as no Scottish version of the

INTRODUCTION.

the Welsh, the Cornish, which is now extinct, and the Armorican or Breton, spoken in the province of Brittany, the ancient Armorica.

Of the Indian division, the most important is the Sanskrit, a language which flourished several centuries before the age of Solomon, and which exhibits a striking resemblance to English, some of the most useful vocables being almost identical in each language. For more than two thousand years Sanskrit has ceased to exist as a spoken idiom, and it is now employed as the official language of the priesthood, as the medium of literature, and is taught in the Brahmanic schools. Its most valuable memorials are the four Vedas, the Brahmanic Scriptures. Its lineal descendants are the Prakit and Pali dialects, which in their turn were succeeded by the languages now spoken in Hindostan; the Hindostani; the Bengali; and Marathi. The varying dialects of the Gypsies are manifestly related to the Indian family.

The Persian or Iranian class includes, First, the Zend, preserved in the Avesta, or Zend Avesta, the sacred writings, and its home is supposed to have been the country known as Bactria; Second, the

---

Scriptures was ever authorized. John Knox and his associates were accused of Anglicizing in their language as well as in their politics, and Ninian Winzet, the Popish antagonist of Knox, was the last who wrote the language in its purity. The union of the crowns, in the succeeding century, reduced Scotland to the condition of a mere province, but left it in possession of a noble literature, the product of two centuries which had intervened from Barbour to James VI., the last of the Scottish kings, and who may be considered the last of the Scottish poets in more senses than one. The Scottish dialect was formed under the same influences as the English; its characteristics are familiar to the readers of Burns and Sir Walter Scott. Many of the difficulties of Shakspere's English receive their successful elucidation in this dialect.

old Persian, which is found in the cuneiform inscriptions by which the conquerors of the East endeavoured to transmit the record of their achievements. Third, the modern Persian, which has been simplified by the loss of its inflections, and has received large accessions of Arabic words.

To this class may also be referred the language of the Kurds, the Afghans, and the ancient and the modern Armenians. The cultivated dialectic varieties of ancient Greek were the Æolic, the Ionic, the Doric, and the Attic. The Attic, by superior culture, attained the pre-eminence, and became the general speech of cultivated society. The Greek was succeeded by the Romaic or modern Greek, which has experienced a simplification of structure somewhat similar to that of Anglo-Saxon in its transition into English. The Latin, in the classic form in which it has descended to us, exhibits the dialect of books, and of the educated Romans from about a century before the Christian Era. It was one of a number of Italian dialects, over which it gradually acquired the ascendency. Its modern descendants, the Romance (Roman) languages, are the Italian, the Spanish, the Portuguese, the Provençal, formerly the language of South France, Langue D'Oc, the French proper, formerly spoken in Northern France, Langue D'Oyl; the Wallachian, spoken in the Turkish provinces of Wallachia and Moldavia (northern Turkey), but largely interpenetrated with Sclavonic words; the Catalan, spoken in Spain, and generally classed as a dialect of the Spanish, though its linguistic position is independent; the Rhæto-Romanic or Roumansch, spoken in Southern Switzerland and around the head of the Adriatic Sea. The term Romance, as the designation of these languages, may be traced to the

Lingua Rustica Romana or Popular Latin, upon which they are principally based. The oldest member of the Sclavonic family is the ancient Bulgarian, commonly known as the Church Sclavic, or Sclavonic, and still the sacred language of the Greek Church. The most widely diffused branch is the Russian, which has two divisions, the Russian proper and the little Russian, the latter including the Servian, the Croatian, and Slavonian. The others are the Polish, the Bohemian, the Moravian, the Slovakian, the Sorbian, and the Polatian, spoken on the Elbe. The Polish language began to be cultivated in the fourteenth century, and it was at one time the vehicle of a flourishing literature, which perished with the extinction of Polish nationality. The Lithuanic or Lettic family includes the old Prussian formerly spoken in northeastern Prussia, and now superseded by the Low German. The Lithuanian and the Lettish are still in use among the inhabitants of the Russian and Prussian provinces along the Baltic Sea, but are rapidly yielding to the encroachments of the German and the Russian, and seem destined to speedy extinction. During the year 1871 there was a decree issued by the Russian Government, prohibiting the use of the German, and prescribing the employment of the Russian within the Baltic provinces of Russia. The Indo-European or Aryan family is not restricted to a circumscribed area, but is exposed to the influence of other tongues, to some of which it is geographically related. In the present state of linguistic science the true position and relation of all the languages of Europe is not ascertained.

The Etruscan, spoken in ancient Etruria (Tuscany), is still the puzzle of philologists; the Basque, spoken on each side of the Pyrenees, is of Aquitanian and Iberian origin. On its northern boundary the Aryan family touches the Turanian or Altaic class, comprehending the languages of the Manchoos, the Mongols, the Asiatic and the European Turks, the Magyars in Hungary, the Finns, and the Laplanders. On its southeastern frontier it comes into contact with the Dravidian or Tamulian group, spoken in the Deccan or southern part of the peninsula of India. In southwestern Asia it meets the Semitic class, including the ancient Hebrew, the sacred language of Israel, the Aramaic, spoken in Syria, Mesopotamia, Babylonia, and Assyria, and perpetuated chiefly in its two dialects, the Syriac and the Chaldee. The Aramaic was in common use among the Jews at the advent of Christianity, having been adopted by them during the Babylonish captivity for the purposes of literary composition, as well as of conversation. It possesses for us a peculiar interest, being the language which was spoken by our Lord and his disciples.*

---

* For information respecting the other linguistic families of the earth, the student is referred to the excellent works of Prof. Max Müller and Prof. Whitney.

HISTORY

OF THE

ENGLISH LANGUAGE.

CHAPTER I.

ANGLO-SAXON PERIOD.   A. D. 449–A. D. 1066.

The Teutonic Invasions of Britain. The History of the English Language commences with the Anglo-Saxon invasions of Britain, about the middle of the fifth century of the Christian Era.* By the term Anglo-Saxon, we are not to understand any particular tribe or nation, or any definite number of tribes or clans. The word is

---

* The *commencement* of the Germanic invasions of Britain was probably long anterior to the middle of the fifth century of the Christian era. It was from this period that these invasions assumed a formidable and organized character, but that the Germanic tribes had found their way into the island before this time is obvious from the following facts: "First. At the conclusion of the Marcomannic war, Marcus Antoninus transplanted a number of Germans into Britain. Second. Alemannic auxiliaries served along with Roman legions under Valentinian. Third. The Notitia Utriusque Imperii, of which the latest date is half a century earlier than the epoch of Hengist, mentions as an officer of state, the *Comes litoris Saxonici, per Britannias:* his government extending along the coast from Portsmouth to the Wash."—*Latham.*

employed with the same latitude of meaning that we attach to the word *Indians*, and is merely a convenient designation of those Teutonic hordes which poured into Britain from about the middle of the fifth century to the middle of the sixth. The Celts, the original inhabitants of the island, were subdued but not extirpated by the invaders, who became a powerful nationality, and called themselves Aenglisc or English; the country they called Aengla-land, the land of the Angles, or England. * It is difficult to determine the nationality of the various tribes by which Britain was gradually colonized. The Anglo-Saxon tongue cannot be identified with any existing Continental speech, nor can the nation be traced to any particular tribes or clans whose names history has recorded. There is abundant linguistic evidence of a great blending of dialects and tribes in the body of invaders; the Anglo-Saxon was not a harmonious or symmetrical language, but revealed even in its purest stages the diversity of elements which had entered into its composition. Its etymologies were defective in clearness, its syntax was discordant, its inflections lacked the regularity that characterizes the Latin. Every feature of the language indicated a diversity, not a unity of origin, and we may safely conclude that both language and people were formed by the fusion of many dialects and clans in proportions which cannot be accurately determined, and whose geographical position comprehended all that part of Germany between the Rhine and the Eider, with the contiguous countries, Holland and Denmark. The Angles were probably of Danish origin, or at least Low German. They were thus related to the Jutes, who settled Kent and the Isle of Wight. The large Scandinavian element among the conquerors of

Britain has not been noted with that degree of attention to which its importance entitles it. The presence of this infusion of Scandinavian blood is attested, First. By the Danish or Scandinavian vocables and constructions which the English language has retained. Second. By the numerous Runic monuments that have been discovered in Scandinavia and in England, while none have been brought to light upon German soil.

The Angles spread themselves over the north and east of England, and it is plausibly conjectured that the course of their conquests sustained some relation to their original position upon the Continent. The population of Northumbria, or the kingdoms north of the Humber, of East Anglia, and of Kent, may thus be assigned to the borderlands of Denmark and Germany.* This semi-Scandinavian origin is corroborated by the vigorous and enterprising spirit of the race, who have contributed powerfully to the development of English prosperity and greatness. The origin of the Saxons is not so easily explained. Essex, Sussex, Wessex, East Saxons, South Saxons, West Saxons, testify by their names to Saxon settlements. "From their strong nationality, which carried them through so many wars, they seem to have been a people, and not a mere federation. From their language, from their seafaring life, from their great aptitude for dyke-making, and from the distinct evidence of Procopius, who calls them Friesians, it would seem natural to refer them to the districts of Holland and North Germany, between the mouths of the Eider and the Rhine." The relationship subsisting between the Saxons, Hollanders, and Friesians, is perhaps more strikingly illustrated by lin-

---

* Pearson's "England in the Middle Ages."

guistic evidence. Among all the tongues of Europe, none display so marked a resemblance to the English as the Hollandish or Dutch, the Low German, and the Friesian. This is rendered obvious by noticing the many points of resemblance in pronunciation and in vocabulary, which exist between the Friesian and the South-English, of which Anglo-Saxon constitutes the basis.

The Saxons extended their dominion over the south and the west of the island, peaceably coalescing with the Angles in the east, from whom they were separated by no differences either in language or in civilization so marked as to prevent their harmonious blending. Thus all England passed into the possession of a new population, except the inaccessible northern and western portions. Mercia, or the March (boundary) country, formed the boundary line of the great nationalities which divided this fair land.*

The Anglo-Saxon Language.

From what has been said, it is evident that the Anglo-Saxon was a composite tongue, formed by the gradual

---

* The settlements of Britain by the Germanic invaders are said to have occurred in the following order :

First. Jutes, under Hengist and Horsa, who occupied Kent and the Isle of Wight and a part of Hampshire, in A. D. 449 or 450. *Second.* The first division of the Saxons, under Ella and Cissa, settled in Sussex in 477. *Third.* The second body of Saxons, under Cerdic and Cymric, in Wessex in 495. *Fourth.* The third body of Saxons in Essex in 530. *Fifth.* First division of the Angles in the Kingdom of East Anglia (Norfolk, Suffolk, Cambridgeshire, and parts of Lincolnshire and Northamptonshire). *Sixth.* The second division of the Angles in the kingdom of Beornicia (situated between the Tweed and the Frith of Forth), in 547.—*Morris's Outlines of English Accidence.*

blending of many kindred dialects, principally introduced into the island between the middle of the fifth and the middle of the sixth century, with a copious infusion of Latin derived from the Romanized Britons. The Anglo-Saxon was an inflected or synthetic language, like the Latin and the Greek. Although at the epoch of its most flourishing literature, its rich inflectional system had been somewhat reduced by the action of sound decay, a result which may be partly attributed to the Danish invasions, it retained a full set of terminations and great freedom of arrangement. With respect to its grammar, it is sufficient to say that it had five cases—that the article, noun, adjective, and pronoun were declinable, having different forms for three genders and two numbers: the adjective, as in German, had two inflections, the definite and the indefinite; the verb had four moods, the indicative, subjunctive, imperative, and infinitive, and but two tenses, the present or indefinite, used also as a future, and the past. There were also compound tenses in the active voice, and a passive voice, formed, as in English, by auxiliaries. The auxiliaries usually retained their force as independent verbs, and were not employed as mere indications of time, as in English. The Anglo-Saxon had ten forms for the article, five for the noun, and ten terminations for the positive degree of adjectives; the irregular verbs had thirteen endings, without including the inflected cases of the participles.

In all the loftier attributes of speech the Anglo-Saxon was the peer of any of the cognate Gothic languages. Though inferior to the Icelandic in the mere devices of rhetoric, in metrical and rhythmical appliances, it was perfectly adequate to the expression of the varied necessities of humanity. Its native roots possessed a remarkable facility of composition and derivation, though the number of its primitive and simple words was so great that there was less occasion for composition than in most of the related languages.

This characteristic, together with the mode of inflection employed, will explain in a measure the large monosyllabic element existing in Anglo-Saxon, and consequently in English; a peculiarity of our tongue which has been forcibly illustrated by the late Dr. Joseph Addison Alexander, of Princeton, in the sonnet here quoted. It will be observed that nearly every word is of Anglo-Saxon derivation, and that those consisting of two syllables are usually enunciated as one.

> Think not that strength lies in the big, round word,
>   Or that the brief and plain must needs be weak.
> To whom can this be true who once has heard
>   The cry for help, the tongue that all men speak,
> When want, or fear, or woe, is in the throat,
>   So that each word gasped out is like a shriek
> Pressed from the sore heart, or a strange, wild note,
>   Sung by some fay or fiend? There is a strength,
> Which dies if stretched too far, or spun too fine,
>   Which has more height than breadth, more depth than length;
> Let but this force of thought and speech be mine,
>   And he that will, may take the sleek, fat phrase,
> Which glows, but burns not, though it beam and shine,
>   Light, but no heat—a flash, but not a blaze.

The Anglo-Saxon language attained its pre-eminence during the reign of King Alfred (870–901). Under the fostering care of this royal scholar, the speech of Wessex attained an ascendency among the dialects of England, similar to that which the Attic acquired among the dialects of Hellas. Wessex became the centre of culture, and its language advanced rapidly to the position of a classic and dominant speech. The Anglian or Northumbrian dialect, which at one time contained the germs of a vigorous and hopeful literature, succumbed to the fearful desolations of the Danes, the destruction of the monasteries, and the consequent extinction of learning, and is lost to sight, until it reappears in the fifteenth century as the national speech of Scotland (Lowland Scotch).

Under the reign of Alfred, the Danes are expelled, comparative security is restored, and the literary supremacy passes over to the tongue of the West Saxons. In this language was composed the greatest and the most cultivated portion of Saxon literature. Its grammar is characterized by regularity and uniformity, and its vocabulary is not affected by Scandinavian or Danish terms. The development of the Northumbrian dialect was arrested by the causes already indicated; hence its literary memorials are few. It possesses inflections and words which are not contained in the Wessex dialect, and the number of Danish terms is very few. These are the two forms in which the Anglo-Saxon existed before the Norman conquest, 1066.

The literature of the Anglo-Saxons has exerted no determining influence either upon the form or the spirit of English literature. The English Language and English literature were new creations, and the latter has derived none of its distinctive features from Anglo-Saxon prototypes. The influence of Anglo-Saxon upon English is confined to the vocabulary and the grammar, and does not seriously affect the literature. Hence the discussion of its literary memorials is somewhat irrelevant in this work, the intention of which is to trace the growth of the English *language,* and not the history of English literature, except so far as it illustrates the mutations and vicissitudes of the tongue. The consideration of this subject properly pertains to professed treatises upon English literature.

The Anglo-Saxons never attained the loftiest excellence either in poetry or prose. The poetical compositions are generally of a religious character, and, while destitute of inventive or creative power, are pure and elevated in tone and sentiment, though pervaded by that exuberance of metaphor, and gorgeousness of imagery which characterize the early literature of every people. Metre* and rhyme were not essential features of their versification, though both were occasionally employed, and the introduction of rhyme into English poetry dates from Anglo-Saxon times. The distinctive feature of Anglo-Saxon poetry was alliteration, which it possessed in common with the Old Northern or Icelandic. The rule which determined its employment, stated in general terms, is as follows: "In each couplet, three emphatic words (or by poetic license accented syllables), two in the first line, and one in the second, must commence with the same consonant, or with vowels, in which case the initial letters might be, and generally were, different."

The following lines will illustrate the nature of alliteration, both in vowels and consonants:

        *P*ilgrymes and *p*almeres,
        *P*lighten hem togidere,

---

* The metrical system of the Anglo-Saxons was probably affected by the influence of Icelandic models, as it possesses some metrical features in common with the Icelandic. For example, the Icelandic tended to break down the Anglo-Saxon alliteration, and thus to prepare the way for the introduction of rhyme.

> For to *s*eken *s*cint Jame,
> And *s*eintes at Rome.
> They *w*enten forth in hire *w*ey,
> With many *w*ise tales,
> And hadden *l*eve to *l*yen,
> Al hire *l*if after.

These lines are specimens of alliteration upon a vowel:

> And *i*nobedient to ben *u*nderdone
> Of *a*ny lif lyvynge,
> With *i*nwit and with *o*utwit
> *Y*magynen and studie.

In historical composition, the Anglo-Saxons appear to have been remarkably deficient, presenting in this regard a strange contrast to their brilliant Norman successors, who treasured up the records of their ancestral greatness with the same zealous guardianship that the Greeks and Latins cherished the legends of heroes and demi-gods. The Anglo-Saxon chronicle, which terminates A. D. 1154, is a monotonous recital of unimportant incidents, devoid of constructive skill, or graphic delineation. The genial climate and generous soil of Angleland enervated the martial spirit of the Teutonic barbarians; and after they had subdued the Kelts, the primitive inhabitants, they lapsed into inglorious quietude, rarely rousing themselves to vigorous effort, except when called upon to repel the aggressions of Scandinavian hordes. With the death of Alfred, the greatness of the Anglo-Saxon commonwealth began to wane, literature declined, social and artistic culture deteriorated, and only the infusion of a vigorous and buoyant civilization could avert the doom that seemed impending over the Saxon

State. Whence this restoring element was to come we shall learn hereafter.

When the Anglo-Saxons invaded Britain, the Romans, who had held the island since the reign of Vespasian,* had been recently called away from this outpost of the Empire to the defence of their own capital against the formidable encroachments of the northern barbarians. Hence the country reverted to the possession of its ancient inhabitants, who enjoyed a brief interval of freedom before they were transferred to the dominion of their new sovereigns. There is no historical foundation for the prevalent opinion that the Kelts were gradually extirpated by their Saxon conquerours. The large number of familiar terms in the vocabulary of the English language, of Keltic origin, the names of rivers, mountains, hills, and towns, which have descended from the same source, ought effectually to dispel the popular impression that the Keltic nation was entirely exterminated by the Teutonic tribes. The Saxon conquest was rather conservative than destructive in its tendencies. The maritime life of the Saxons naturally inclined them to the sea, and consequently we discover that the largest Saxon settlements are found in maritime districts. For a long time the Saxons were averse to city life, and restricted themselves to those regions which the sea washes. Still a certain degree of contact

---

* The Roman invasions of Britain were commenced by Julius Cæsar, B. C. 55. His invasion accomplished no substantial result, and it was not until repeated contests, continued during several reigns, that the island was rendered subject to Rome. The conquest was completed under the beneficent administration of Agricola, A. D. 78–86. The Roman legions were finally withdrawn in the reign of Valentinian, A. D. 447.

and admixture with the native population was inevitable. "If the Roman towns in some cases fell into decay, the poverty of a war-stricken people, the decline of commerce and of the arts, will account for it. But the days of the great Roman feasts were still celebrated under Christian titles, the Roman colleges of trade were continued as guilds. Roman local names were preserved by the conquerours, as they found them. Roman titles, duke and count, were assumed by the Saxon chiefs. Roman law has formed the basis of the Saxon family system, and of the laws of property. The Saxon conquest was a change of the highest moment, no doubt, but it did not break up society; it only added a new element to what it found. The Saxon State was built upon the ruins of the past."*

The Saxons, however, were not permitted to enjoy in tranquil security the possession of their conquered territory. About the beginning of the ninth century, commenced the fearful incursions of the Scandinavian pirates, who were the terror and the scourge of Europe, and from whose depredations immunity was generally secured by exorbitant ransom, or enormous concessions. One branch of the Northmen or Norsemen desolated the kingdom of Gaul, and obtained from that imbecile monarch, Charles the Simple, the cession of one of his fairest provinces, Neustria, known henceforth in history as Normandy, from its new inhabitants. Of them we shall have more to say directly, as they play a brilliant part in the history of the English language and the English race. Another division sailed towards Angleland, and thus laid the foundations for the conquests of their

---

* Pearson's "England in the Middle Ages."

kinsmen in the ages to come. This was the first great act of the Scandinavian races, in the drama of European history.

The Danish invasions and occupations of England may be stated in the following order:

In 787 the Northmen * appeared, and made an attack upon the coast of Dorsetshire. In 832 the Danes ravaged Sheppey in Kent. In 833 thirty-five ships came to Charmouth in Dorsetshire, and Egbert was defeated by the Danes. In 835 the Welsh and Danes were defeated by Egbert at Hengestesdun. In 855 the Danes wintered in Sheppey. In 866 they wintered in East Anglia. In 868 they got into Mercia as far as Nottingham, and in 870 they invaded East Anglia. In 871 the eastern part of Wessex was invaded by the Danes. In 874 the Danes entered Lincolnshire. In 876 they made settlements in Northumbria. In 878 Alfred, King of Wessex, concluded a treaty with Guthrum, the Danish chief, and formally ceded to the invaders all Northumberland and East Anglia, the greater part of Essex, and the northeast of Mercia. In 991 the Norwegians invaded the eastern coast of England, and plundered Ipswich; they were defeated at the battle of Maldon. Before 1000 the Danes had settled in Cumberland. In 1013 Svein, King of Denmark, conquered England; and from 1013 to 1042 a Danish dynasty ruled over England. In 1042 the government reverted to the possession of the Anglo-Saxons, who retained it until the Norman Conquest, 1066. The free spirit of the

---

* The terms Northmen, Norsemen, or Scandinavians, are the general designations of the inhabitants of Scandinavia (Norway, Sweden, and Denmark), who at that time were called Danes, without distinction.

Danes exercised a salutary influence upon the political and social condition of the Saxon State.

Under the paternal government of Canute, the Danish aristocracy coalesced with the Anglo-Saxon; <u>the difference in language and race was not so great as to render union impossible, and when the government was restored to the Anglo-Saxons, upon the overthrow of the Danish power,</u> those Danes who desired it retained undisturbed possession of their homes, and became subjects of the Saxon rulers.

CHAPTER II.

THE NORMAN CONQUEST.

The battle of Hastings, fought October 14, 1066, transferred the kingdom of England to the government of William, Duke of Normandy, and his followers. We have already learned that the Normans were originally a branch of the great Scandinavian family to which the Danes belonged, and that in the tenth century they had wrested from the King of France one of his loveliest provinces. Henceforth their character undergoes an entire transformation. Laying aside their natural rudeness, and discarding their Scandinavian dialect, they entered boldly upon that wonderful career which was to make them the foremost among the nations of mediæval history. Possessed of a susceptible and versatile genius, they rapidly advanced from a condition of barbarism to comparative civilization and enlightenment. They readily acquired the speech of the land, a language formed by the decay and corruption of the *Lingua Rustica*, or popular Latin, the colloquial dialect of the Empire, which had been disseminated throughout the Roman provinces by the legionaries, the tradesmen, and the colonists. In France it had assumed two separate forms, distinguished by the word for *yes* in each tongue, a manner of designating languages by no means uncommon in the Middle ages. These are known in history and in philology as the Langue D'Oc, or Provençal, the tongue of south France, once the favourite medium of the Troubadours; the Langue D'Oyl, or northern French, with which the Norman French is identified. The river Loire may be considered the dividing line between them. The southern French, or Langue D'Oc, exhibits a marked resemblance to the dialects of Spain; the northern French, or Langue D'Oyl, which extends from the Loire to the boundaries of Flanders, differs in certain respects from the Langue D'Oc. First. It was of later origin, southern Gaul having been conquered at an earlier period by the Romans. Second. It contains a Germanic element, as by its geographical position it is brought into contact with the Gothic languages of Holland and Germany, and northern France was colonized by Teutonic tribes in the fifth century. This Germanic element is quite important. Third. It contains a Scandinavian element, as the Normans retained some of their original words after they had abandoned their former tongue. Fourth. It has a number of Keltic words, some of which were introduced into England by the Normans, and are perpetuated in the English language.

The northern French assumed several dialectic forms, determined by the phonetic tendencies of the different tribes and nationalities among whom it was spoken. These were the dialects of Picardy, of Normandy, of the Isle of France, and of Burgundy. They were all originally upon a footing of linguistic equality, but during the fourteenth century the speech of the Isle of France attained the pre-eminence, in consequence of the political ascendency acquired by those who spoke it, and became the standard or literary language. The others descended to the level of mere patois, or uncultivated dialects.* It is with the dialect of Normandy that we are directly concerned, as the literary French exercised no specific influence upon English until the reign of Edward III. The Norman French was, as we have already seen, a Franco-Roman dialect, formed from the rude Latin of Gaul, containing a strong German admixture, as well as a Scandinavian and a Celtic element. It was characterized by great simplicity of form and structure, a feature which is conspicuously displayed in its preference for single vowels and single consonants. Its pronunciation is supposed to have borne a strong resemblance to that of Anglo-Saxon, which may perhaps serve to explain the fusion of two tongues so essentially different, a fact unparalleled in linguistic history.

The Norman tongue was not totally unknown in England before the Conquest. This will appear from the following historical facts. We discover repeated in-

---

* As *patois* and *dialect* will occur again in this work, and as they are used frequently as synonymous or convertible terms, it may be well to explain the difference before proceeding further. A dialect, properly defined, is one of several independent and equal forms of a language. In point of literary merit they may be peers. Thus, the speech of Burgundy, Picardy, Normandy, and the Isle of France were cognate and equal dialects of the Langue D'Oyl, until the last secured the ascendency, and the others sunk to mere patois. Dialects, accurately understood, exist in the earlier stages of a language, before superior culture or political predominance has elevated one tribe or nationality and its language above the others. Patois, then, are those unfortunate dialects which, excelled by their competitors in the struggle for literary honours, have become the speech of the peasant and the brogue of the rural districts.

For accurate and detailed information upon these points, the student is referred to Brachét's "Historical Grammar of French;" Littré's "History of the French Language," in his magnificent dictionary.

stances of intercourse between the two countries before this time: First. The residence in England of Louis Outremer. Second. Ethelred II. married Emma, daughter of Richard, Duke of Normandy, and the two children were sent to Normandy to be educated. Third. Edward the Confessor possessed a peculiar predilection for the Normans; during his reign the offices of state were filled by Norman favourites; the Norman tongue was cultivated in England, and French manners and customs became fashionable among the higher circles. He has been appositely called the first of the Norman monarchs of England. Fourth. Ingulphus, of Croydon, speaks of his knowledge of French. Fifth. Harold, the last of the Saxon kings, spent some time in Normandy with William. Sixth. William of Normandy visited England, and was received with all the splendor of a king by Edward. Seventh. The French article *la*, in the term *la Drove*, occurs in a deed of A. D. 975.

The Norman Conquest removed England from her isolated position, and introduced her into the sphere of Continental relations. It appears to have been the uniform policy of the Conquerour to leave the existing laws and institutions unaltered, and content himself with their rigourous enforcement. Notwithstanding the proscriptive and vindictive spirit by which some of his measures were actuated, his administration was attended with substantial benefits, and succeeded in effecting a political unity hitherto unknown in England. The character and condition of English society experienced a total transformation. The Normans constituted but a small proportion of the population, and they never transferred themselves generally or in a body to England. But their political and social predominance, more than counteracted their limited numbers; they rapidly acquired all positions of honour and emolument, in church and state. Norman prelates supplanted the Saxon bishops, the avenues to honour and distinction were closed against all but the adherents of the Conquerour, and no man could attain to eminence except by becoming, in speech and in manners, a Frenchman. The native language and literature, which had been deteriorating since the age of Alfred, fell into neglect and decay; excluded from the schools, from the church, from elegant and courtly circles, it rapidly declined, though it never ceased entirely to be cultivated, during the long period of its depression that intervened between the Conquest and the time of Chaucer. It remained the vernacular tongue of the people, who cherished it all the more ardently on account of its misfortunes, and in the cloisters of the Saxon monks it was guarded with assiduous care, and preserved from utter literary extinction.

Its productions were naturally imperfect; nearly all of our Anglo-Saxon literature, from the Conquest to the time that it was kindled into life under the inspiration of Chaucer, consists of translations and paraphrases, a circumstance which forcibly indicates the absence of original genius, and literary patronage. The decline of Saxon letters and learning had commenced before the Conquest. It is true that this event greatly accelerated the process, but it was not the original cause. When the Normans invaded England, the Anglo-Saxons were reduced to the lowest degree of ignorance and illiteracy.

Odericus Vitalis, a native of England, and almost contemporary with the events he describes, speaks of his countrymen as having been found by the Normans, "a rustic and almost illiterate people," a remark which applies especially to the clergy, as the great body of the laity were everywhere illiterate. The Conquerour took advantage of this prevailing ignorance of the clergy to deprive many of them of their benefices, and to supply their places with Norman favourites, many of whom were accomplished scholars.

Upon the whole, it cannot be affirmed that the Norman Conquest was unfavourable to the interest of learning and of civilization. "William himself," says Warton (History of English Poetry), "patronized and loved letters. He filled the bishoprics and abbacies of England with the most learned of his countrymen, who had been educated at the University of Paris, at that time the most flourishing school in Europe. He placed Lanfranc, Abbot of the monastery of St. Stephen, at Caen, in the See of Canterbury—one of the most eminent logicians of that age. Anselm, an acute metaphysician and theologian, his immediate successor in the same See, was called from the government of the Abbey of Bec in Normandy." The speculations of these eminent dialecticians had "almost reconstructed philosophical opinion in Europe." William and his nobles founded and endowed some of the most magnificent institutions of learning in England, and he patronized liberally all enterprises designed to promote the interests of culture, or to foster and develop a love for letters. He set the example himself, by educating his own son, Henry Beauclerc, with the utmost care, in all the sciences known and studied in this age of comparative ignorance. Many of his successors manifested the same respect for learning; many of them had received the most thorough education which was then afforded. Still, whatever learning existed, was in a great degree the exclusive possession of the clergy, and but few even of the nobility seem to have been versed in the scholarship of the age. The Latin tongue, which was then the general medium of all knowledge, was unknown except to the clergy, and to such of the laity as had embraced the profession of teaching.

There long existed a prevalent misapprehension that the Norman Conquerour endeavoured to force upon his new subjects the language of Normandy, and thus to effect the total abolition of the Saxon speech. Hume tells us that "the Conquerour entertained the difficult project of abolishing the English language, and for that purpose he ordered that, in all schools throughout the kingdom, the youth should be instructed in the French tongue. The pleadings in the supreme court of judicature were in French, the deeds were drawn in the same language, the laws were composed in the same idiom." This statement must be received with decided modifications. It is true that French was the language of the court and of genteel society from infancy; that boys in the grammar schools were taught to translate and construe their Latin into French; and so fashionable had the use of it become that even rustic and uncouth persons endeavoured to speak French, in order "to be thought something of," into such neglect and contempt had the Saxon speech fallen. The mass of the people, however, adhered pertinaciously to their native speech. With regard to the remainder of this assertion, so general in its character, it may be said that later and more accurate historical researches have shown that there is no one example of any pleadings in the court of judicature in French, of any deeds or charters drawn in the same language, or any laws composed in that idiom, until the reign of Henry III. "What William found he kept;

like his predecessors, his charters were written either in English or Latin, though the latter gradually prevailed. Yet the English continued in constant use, and the last example of its employment is found also in the reign of Henry III., when we had the first employment of the French tongue. * * * * No doubt the Romance dialect prevailed greatly in England in later times, but for this we cannot hold William responsible, and every letter, every writ, every missive which he addressed to his trusty men—his Frenchmen or his Englishmen—was in Latin or in English. It was not until the conclusion of Henry III.'s reign that the Norman-French appears in the monuments of our jurisprudence and diplomacy."* He even undertook to learn the language of his Saxon subjects, in order that he might be qualified to decide suits at law, to which they were parties. The difficulty of the undertaking, however, induced him to abandon it; the Norman lords could not acquire the correct pronunciation of Saxon words, they mutilated its local names,† and their sovereign probably experienced the same difficulty. There is no historical evidence whatever for the assertion so frequently repeated, that the Norman Conquerour designed the destruction of the Saxon tongue; such a result would have been unattainable except by the extirpation of the race who spoke it; and the decline and neglect of Saxon speech and Saxon letters were rather accelerated than directly produced by the Conquest; they did not proceed from deliberate policy, or royal interdiction; the same result was inevitable in any event, even if the Normans had never set foot in England.

---

* Palgrave's "England and Normandy."
† For example, they pronounced *Lincoln, Nicole.*

CHAPTER III:

THE INFLUENCE OF THE NORMAN CONQUEST UPON THE ANGLO-SAXON TONGUE.

THE decline of Anglo-Saxon speech and literature had commenced, as we have learned, long before the era of the Conquest. The first perceptible effect of Norman-French upon Anglo-Saxon was to impart a stimulus to that process of decomposition or phonetic decay,*

---

* Phonetic decay is that process of decomposition or disintegration which is ever active in language, but which is more violent in its operations at some periods than at others. It is produced by vocal relaxation, careless and indistinct pronunciation, such as we habitually listen to, the slurring over or suppressing of syllables, the dropping of consonants between two vowels, the abbreviation and mutilation of long words, in order to avoid the trouble of enunciating them clearly; in a word, it comprehends all those expedients to which we unconsciously resort, in order to economize the breath; it is the practical or utilitarian element in speech, and by its agency many of the most important transmutations of language have been effected. Familiar examples of it are, *don't* for *do not*, *shan't* for *shall not*, *can't* for *cannot*, etc. The greater part of the changes that occurred in the transition of Saxon into English, are attributable to its agency.

Thus: A. S. hafoc in English became hawk.
" dacg in " " day.
" sprecan in " " speak.
" morgen in " " morrow.
" cyning in " " king.
" hláford in " " lord.
" sælig in " " silly.

which had already begun to assail the integrity of the tongue, and to transmute it from an inflected or synthetic language to an uninflected or analytic speech. Had there been no Norman Conquest, it is probable that Saxon would have experienced a decided simplification of structure, such as nearly all the languages of the Low German stock have undergone. This had been already partially accomplished in the north and east of England by the influence of the Danish invasions. The inherent tendency of all languages to simplification of structure, would in the course of time have produced this result, but without the Conquest, it would have been much more gradual, and by no means so complete. The first perceptible change produced by the Conquest effected the orthography; the vocabulary received no decided modification until a much later period. The Norman-French, for a century after the occupation of England, experienced no important change; its orthography and some of its forms were slightly altered, but it remained essentially unimpaired until a subsequent period.

Latin, as was the case everywhere throughout Europe during the dark and middle ages, continued to be the dialect of the Church and of learning; French the speech of the foreigners; while the mass of the native population retained with invincible tenacity their vernacular tongue. The fact that it had ceased to be generally cul-

---

A. S. wif-man in English became woman.
" Eofor-wick in " " York.
" hlæfdige in " " lady.
" bren-ston in " " brimstone-burnstone.
" nawiht in " " nought.
" secgan in " " say. [the nail.
" angnægele in " " hangnail,—a sore under

tivated, greatly facilitated the process of phonetic decay, and consequent simplification of structure. The conservative influence of culture no longer restrained or retarded its action; the pronunciation became corrupt, terminations disappeared, the constitution of the speech was infected with a malady which nothing could relieve but an entire reconstruction, or a transmutation of its form and character. There being no longer any generally acknowledged standard of literary excellence, the language lost whatever uniformity it had once possessed, and the germs of dialectic divergence began to be developed. The two idioms remained side by side without intermingling;* a natural effect of the animosities and distrust which the Conquest had generated. Still the necessities of intercourse, however limited, between conquerors and conquered, gradually produced a kind of mixed dialect, composed of a blending of French and Saxon, and popularly known as "Marlborough French," resembling the Lingua Franca of the Levant, or the slang of Anglo-Indian society, utterly confounding the two vocabularies, and disregarding grammatical forms.†

Important to be noticed among the changes produced by French influence are the following: *C* before the Conquest was pronounced hard, like K. Its present soft s-sound, also the softened forms *ch*, *sh*, are due to the French influence: *g* is often changed to *w* and *y*, which is due to the same cause; through the agency of the

---

* For a considerable period after the Conquest, the French was probably principally spoken in the large towns and cities, in which the Normans mostly resided. The Anglo-Saxon prevailed generally in the villages, and in the rural districts, where comparatively few Normans congregated.

† Pearson's "England in the Middle Ages."

French, the *th*, 3d person singular Indic. Pres., was gradually softened to *s*. Under the same influence *s*, which was a favorite plural termination of French nouns, became the generally received sign of the plural in English.

All the phenomena of linguistic history may be classified under two heads: dialectic convergence, and dialectic divergence. The evolutions of language are confined to these processes of concentration and dispersion.* Thus, for example, one nationality or tribe secures a political ascendency, or excels its neighbours in literary culture, acquiring for its dialect a pre-eminence, as the standard of correctness, and the medium of literary composition. The others, surpassed in the contest for the supremacy, sink down to mere patois. This is a case of dialectic convergence, and the dialects of Wessex and of the Isle of France may be cited as illustrations. If, on the other hand, the dialect which has attained the superiority, is by some internal convulsion, foreign conquest, or admixture, corrupted, disintegrated; and finally, losing its stability, and uniformity of structure, resolves itself into several dialectic forms, we have an example of divergence. Such a divergence was effected by the breaking up of the ancient Latin into its different Romance descendants; and by the gradual disruption of Anglo-Saxon produced by the Conquest, which caused the language in the twelfth, thirteenth, and fourteenth centuries, to resolve itself into three distinct varieties; viz., the Northern, the Middle, and the Southern dialects.†

---

* Whitney's "Language and the Study of Language."

† The student will find a lively and graphic description of these dialects in Trevisa's translation of Higden's "Polychronicon." Morris's "Specimens of Early English," page 338. The outline of the dialects given in the text, is condensed from Morris.

Their geographical area was as follows: The Northern dialect was spoken throughout the Lowlands of Scotland, Northumberland, Durham, and Yorkshire. The Midland dialect was spoken in all the Midland counties, in the East Anglian counties, and in Cumberland, Westmoreland, Lancashire, and Shropshire. The Southern dialect was spoken in all the counties south of the Thames, in Somersetshire, Gloucestershire, and in parts of Herefordshire, and Worcestershire. These dialects may be distinguished from one another by the employment of different grammatical forms. A convenient test for the illustration of these differences, is found in the inflection of the verb in the present plural indicative.

The Southern dialect employs *eth*, the Midland *en*, as the inflection for all forms of the plural present indicative. The Northern dialect uses neither of these forms, but substitutes *es* for *eth* or *en*. The Northern dialect has its imperative plural in *es*; the Southern and Midland in *eth*. The Midland dialect being widely extended, had various local forms. The most marked of these are: the Eastern Midland, spoken in Lincolnshire, Norfolk, and Suffolk; the West Midland, spoken in Cumberland, Westmoreland, Lancashire, Cheshire, and Shropshire. The East Midland conjugated its verb in the present singular indicative, like the Southern dialect.

    1st person, hop-*e*, I hope.
    2d " hope-*st*, thou hopest.
    3d " hop-*eth*, he hopes.

The West Midland, like the Northern, conjugated its verb as follows:

    1st person, hope.
    2d " hop-*es*.
    3d " hop-*es*.

INFLUENCE OF THE NORMAN CONQUEST. 45

There are other points of difference to be noted. The Southern dialect frequently substituted *v*, where the others used *f*, as *vinger* = finger. It preferred the palatal *ch* to the guttural *k*, in many words; as *riche* = Northern *rike* = kingdom; *crouch* = *croke* = cross. It often had *ō* and *u* where the Northern dialect had *ā* and *i*, as *hul* = Northern *hil*, *put* = Northern pit; *bôn* = Northern ban = bone. In its grammar, the Southern dialect was still more distinctly marked. First. It preserved a large number of nouns with plurals in *n*, as *sterren* = stars, *eyren* = eggs, *kun* = kine. The Northern dialect had only about four of these plurals, viz.: *eghen* = eyes, *hosen*, *oxen*, and *schoon* = shoes. Second. It kept up the genitive of feminine nouns in *e*, while the Northern dialect employed only the masculine suffix *s*, as in modern English. Third. Genitive plurals in *ene* are very common, but do not occur at all in the Northern dialect. Fourth. Adjectives and demonstrative pronouns retained many of the older inflections, and the definite article was inflected. Many pronominal forms were employed in South England, that were never used in the North. Fifth. Where the Anglo-Saxon had infinitives ending in *an* and *ian*, the Southern dialect had *en* or *e* and *ie*. This inflection does not occur in the Northern dialect. Sixth. Active participles ended in *inde* (*ynde*); in the North in *ande* (*and*). Seventh. Passive participles retained the old prefix *ge* (which was very common in Anglo-Saxon before the Conquest), softened down to *i* or *y;* in the North it was never used. Eighth. It had many verbal inflections that were unknown to the Northern dialect, as *st* (present and past tenses), *en* (plural past indicative); *e* (second person plural past indicative of strong verbs). Ninth. The Northern dialect had many plural forms of nouns that were wholly unknown to the Southern dialect, as *brether*=brethren, *childer*=children, *hend*=hands. Tenth. *That* was used as a demonstrative pronoun, as in English, without reference to gender. In the Southern dialect, *that* was often the neuter of the definite article. Eleventh. *Same* (as, *the same, this same*), was used instead of the Southern *thilke*, modern *thuck, thick*. *Thir, ther* (the plural of the Scandinavian article, the, these), was often used. Twelfth. The pronominal forms were very different. Thus, instead of the Southern *heo* (*hi*, hii)=she, this dialect used *sco, scho*, the older form of our *she*. It rejected the old plural pronouns of the third person, and substituted the plural article, as *thai, thair, thaim* (tham), instead of *hi*, (*heo, hii*), *heore* (*here*), heom (hem), *yhoures, thairs*, as common then as now, were unknown in the South of England. *At*=to, was used as a sign of the infinitive; *sal* and *sud*=*schal* and schuld. The Northern dialect had numerous Scandinavian forms; as, *hethen*, hence=Southern *henne*; *thethen*, thence=Southern *thenne*; *whethen*, whence=Southern whennes.

The East Midland dialect has one peculiarity that has not been found in the other dialects, viz: the coalescence of pronouns with verbs, and even with pronouns, as *caldes*=*calde*+es=called them; *dedes*=*dede*+es=put them; *hes*=*he*+*es*=he+them. The West Midland has its peculiarities, as *ho*=she, *hit*=*its*.

For two or three centuries after the Conquest, the confusion and diversity of dialects, produced by the divergence of which we have spoken, was so great that no one could fairly claim to be considered the standard speech.

The Midland dialect was the most widely extended,

and the one which we might naturally expect would become the standard form of the language. Of its many varieties, the East Midland was by far the most important. As early as the beginning of the thirteenth century it began to receive literary culture, and had lost most of its inflections, so as to become a simple analytic speech, like modern English. This dialect, Anglo-Danian in origin and character, gradually penetrated further and further southward, and ended by supplanting the Southern dialect for the higher purposes of literary composition; Trevisa (1387) being the last writer of eminence who employed it. The steady advance of this dialect from about A. D. 1180 until, in the hands of Wickliffe, Gower, and Chaucer, it attained the ascendency, is one of the great facts of our linguistic history.* In this dialect, not

---

* In Puttenham's "Art of Poetry" (1589), Arber's "Reprints of Early English Authors," the student will find some very instructive remarks concerning the English dialects. Puttenham mentions three dialects—the Northern, Western, and Southern. The Northern was that spoken north of the Trent; the Southern was that south of the Trent, which was also the language of the court, the capital, and the surrounding counties; the Western occupied the same limits to which it is now confined, Gloucestershire, Somersetshire, Wiltshire. "Our maker (poet) therefore at these dayes, shall not follow Piers Plowman, nor Gower, nor Lydgate, nor yet Chaucer, for their language is now out of use with us; neither shall he take the termes of Northern-men, such as they use in dayly talke, whether they be noblemen or gentlemen, or of their best clarkes, all is a matter; nor in effect, any speach used in England, beyond the river of Trent, though no man can deny but that theirs is the purer English Saxon at this day, yet it is not so courtly nor so current as our *Southerne English* is, no more is the far Westerne man's speech; ye shall therefore take the usual speech of the Court, and that of London, and the shires lying about London, within sixty miles, and not much above. I say not this, but that in every shire of England, there be gentlemen and others that speake, but

only the works of Chaucer and his illustrious contemporaries were composed, but also the Ormulum, and the writings of Robert of Brunne (1303), who clearly foreshadows the future of the English Language, and the triumph of the East Midland speech. In his diction, the Romance and Teutonic elements are skilfully adjusted, and many modern idioms and familiar combinations appear for the first time, so that he is not inaptly named the "Patriarch of the new English." In the age of Chaucer, the East Midland had become the speech of London and Oxford, and had probably penetrated south of the Thames into Kent and Surrey. At a subsequent date, the Southern dialect had so far receded before it, as to become rather Western than Southern, and the latter designation was the one applied to the languages which had been adopted as the standard.

---

specially write, as good Southerne as we of Middlesex or Surrey do, but not the common people of every shire, to whom the gentlemen, and also their learned clarkes, do for the most part condescend, but herein we are already ruled by th' English dictionaries, and other books written by learned men.'

CHAPTER IV.

TRANSITION OF SAXON INTO ENGLISH.

It has been stated in a preceding chapter, that phonetic decay had made considerable progress in disintegrating the structure of the Saxon tongue, and in converting it from an inflected to an analytic language, before the Conquest imparted a new impulse to the process of decline, and essentially facilitated its completion. We must now consider in detail the progressive series of changes by which Anglo-Saxon lost its synthetic character, and was transmuted into our simple uninflected English. The first change which occurred, affected the orthography.* This may be seen in documents dating from the beginning of the twelfth century, and it consisted in a general weakening of the terminations of words.

First. The older vowel endings *a*, *o*, *u*, were reduced to *e*. This modified the oblique cases of nouns and adjectives, as well as the nominative, so that the termination

an	became	*en.*	*ra, ru*	became	*re.*
as	"	*es.*	*ena*	"	*ene.*
ath	"	*eth.*	*on*	"	*en.*
um	"	*en.*	*od, ode*	"	*ed, ede.*

---

* This outline of inflectional changes is condensed from Morris. It may be found in his "Specimens of Early English," or his "Outlines of English Accidence."

C or *k* is often changed to *ch* soft, and *g* to *w* and *y*. These changes took place between A. D. 1100 and 1250. Between 1150 and 1200, we note the following changes. First. The indefinite article *an*, *a*, is formed from the numeral. It is often inflected. Second. The definite article becomes þe, þeo, þe, (þat), instead of *se, seo, pæt*. It often loses the former inflections, especially in the feminine. We find þe often used as a plural instead of þa or þo. Third. Nominative plurals of nouns end in *en* or *e*, instead of *a* or *u*, thus conforming to plurals of the *n* declension. Fourth. Plurals in *es* sometimes take the place of those in *en* (*an*), the genitive plural ends in *ene* or *e*, and sometimes in *es*. Fifth. The dative plural (originally *um*) becomes *e* and *en*. Sixth. Some uncertainty begins to appear in the gender of nouns. Seventh. Adjectives manifest a tendency to drop the following case endings: 1st, the genitive singular masculine of the indefinite declension. 2d, the genitive and dative feminine of the indefinite declension. 3d, the plural *en* of the definite declension frequently becomes *e*. Eighth. The dual forms are still in use, though not so common. The datives *him, hem*, are used instead of the accusative. Ninth. New pronominal forms appear, as *ha* = *he, she, they; is* = *her; is* = *them; me* = *one*. Tenth. The *n* in *min, thin*, is often dropped before consonants, but retained in the plural, and in the oblique cases. Eleventh. The infinitive frequently drops the final *n*, as *smelle* = *smellen*, to smell. *To* is sometimes used as the sign of the infinitive. Twelfth. The gerundial or dative of the infinitive ends often in *en* or *e*, instead of *enne* (anne). Thirteenth. The *n* of the passive participle is often dropped. Fourteenth. The present participle ends in *inde*, and is often substituted for the gerundial infinitive, as, to *swiminde* = to *swimene*, = to swim. Fifteenth. *Shall* and *will* begin to be employed as auxiliaries of the future tense. The latter half of the twelfth century was a period of great confusion and diversity. The older forms existed side by side with the new ones that were struggling to supplant them, thus proving that the ancient inflections did not yield the supremacy without a vigorous contest. In this period, we first find the *popular* or *provincial* elements budding forth, many of which afterwards became recognized forms of speech.

These changes occur principally in the Southern dialect. In the other dialects of this period (the East and West Midland) phonetic decay had wrought a more thorough simplification of grammatical structure. Thus, in the Ormulum, which is written in the East Midland dialect, we note these essential changes: First. The definite article is used as in modern English, and *that* is a demonstrative without regard to gender. Second. The gender of substantives is nearly the same as at present. Third. *es* is commonly used as the sign of the plural. Fourth. *es*, singular and plural, has become the ending of the genitive or possessive. Fifth. Adjectives, as in the time of Chaucer, have a final *e* for the older inflections, but *e* is chiefly used, 1st, as a sign of the plural; 2d, to distinguish the definite form of the adjective. Sixth. The forms *they, theirs*, come into use. Seventh. Passive participles drop the prefix *i* (*ge*), as, *cumen* for *icumen*. Eighth. The plural of the present indicative ends in *en* instead of *eth*. Ninth. *Arn=are* for *beoth*. In a work written before the middle of the thirteenth century, containing many forms belonging to the West Midland dialect, we find: First. Articles, nouns, and adjectives, as in the Ormulum. Second. The pronoun *thai* instead of *hi* or *heo*=they; *I* for *Ic* or *Ich*. Third. Passive participles frequently omit the prefix *i*. Fourth. Active participles end in *ande* instead of *inde*. In the conjugation of the verbs we notice important changes: First. The substitution of *es* for *est* in the second person of weak or regular verbs. Second. The dropping of *e* in strong or irregular verbs. Between 1150 and 1250 the Norman-French begins to affect slightly the vocabulary of English.

Changes between 1250–1350.

First. The article still retains some of the older inflections: as, the genitive singular feminine; the accusative masculine; the plural *po* (the nominative being used with all cases of nouns). Second. The confusion in the gender of nouns increases, words becoming neuter that were once masculine or feminine. In the course of time the language lost its grammatical gender, and neuter became the designation of objects without life. Anglo-Saxon had its arbitrary system of grammatical gender, like the other Aryan tongues, and the effacing of these perplexing and fictitious distinctions is one of the happiest changes effected by the Norman-French influence. The change itself is directly due to the disappearance of the inflections, indicating the differences of gender and the consequent disappearance of the differences themselves. Third. Plurals in *en* and *es* are used without distinction. Fourth. The genitive *es* becomes more general, and begins to supersede the older *en* and *c* in old masculine and neuter nouns, and *e* in feminine nouns. Fifth. The dative singular of pronouns begins to drop off; *mi*-self and *thi*-self are often substituted for *meself* and *theself*. Sixth. Dual forms of the personal pronouns disappeared about the close of the thirteenth century. Seventh. A final *e* is used for the sign of the plural of adjectives, and for distinguishing between the definite and indefinite declensions. Eighth. The gerundial infinitive ends in *en* or *e*. Ninth. The ordinary infinitive takes the prefix *to*. Tenth. A few irregular verbs become regular. Present participles in *inge* appear about the beginning of the fourteenth century. During this period, and especially towards its close, the French element begins to enter largely into the vocabulary of English.

Changes between 1350–1460.

During this period the Midland acquires the ascendency, and becomes the standard speech. Words from the Northern and Southern dialects retain their characteristic peculiarities. The following points should be noted with care: First. The plural article *tho* = the; those, is still of frequent occurrence. Second. The *es* in plural and genitive case of substantives is mostly a separate syllable.* Third. The pronouns are *I* for the older *Ic*; *sche* for the old form *heo*; *him, them, whom*, used as datives and accusatives; *oures, youres, heres*, in common use for *oure, youre, here*; thei (they) in general use instead of *hi* (heo); *here* = their, *hem* = them. Fourth. The plurals of verbs in the present and past

---

* The sign of the English possessive, 's, is commonly referred to the ending of the Anglo-Saxon genitive, *es* or *is*. But the latter inflection disappeared almost entirely during the period that we are now considering, and it is at least probable that our possessive sign, 's, is a new and distinct inflectional development such as languages sometimes put forth, even at times when their generative energy has apparently disappeared.

indicative end in *en* or *e*. The imperative plural ends in *eth;* *est* is often used as the inflection of the second person singular preterite of strong and weak verbs. The infinitive ends in *en* or *e*, but this inflection often disappears towards the end of the fourteenth century. The present participle ends usually in *ing* (inge). The passive participle of strong verbs ends in *en* or *e*. The termination *e* requires particular attention. It represents an older vowel ending: *nam-e=nam-a;* or the termination *an, en,* as *withute=withutan.* It represents different inflections, and is used, 1st, as a mark of the plural or definite adjective; 2d, as a mark of adverbs; 3d, as a sign of the infinitive mood, past tense of weak verbs, and imperative mood. About the close of this period, the use of final *e* becomes irregular and unsettled, and the forms of pronouns prevalent in the northern dialect, *their, theirs, them,* are generally used in the others.

CHAPTER V.

THE WORKS OF THE TRANSITION PERIOD.

There are several works that have descended to us from the thirteenth century, which afford, as it were, a pictorial illustration of the process by which Anglo-Saxon gradually evolved itself from its rich inflectional dress, and assumed the simple and graceful drapery of our noble English. These works, though devoid of the loftiest excellence, or of mere literary attractions, are valuable and interesting to the student of the English tongue, as serving to elucidate an important, and perhaps difficult era in its historical development. They therefore merit a somewhat detailed consideration. They are Layamon's "Chronicle of Brutus;" the "Ancren Riwle," the "Ormulum," and "Robert of Gloucester's Chronicle." The language of the first three of these may be termed semi-Saxon, or broken Saxon; that of the last is English, and is the first acknowledged composition in the English tongue. Except the "Ancren Riwle," they are all in verse, a form of language in which the early efforts of every literature are embodied. The work of Layamon "is a versified chronicle of the mythical history of Britain and its ancient kings, dating from the destruction of Troy, and the flight of Æneas, from whom descended Brutus, the founder of the British monarchy, and extending to the reign of Athelstan." The "Brut" or "Chronicle of Britain" is principally, though with many additions, a translation of the French "Brut D' Angleterre" of Wace, a French scholar, which was itself a translation, with considerable additions, of Geoffrey of Monmouth's "Latin History of the Britons," which is also a translation from a French or Welsh original. "So that the genealogy of the four versions is as follows: First, a Celtic original probably, now lost; Secondly, the Latin of Geoffrey of Monmouth; Thirdly, the French of Wace; Fourthly, the English of Layamon." The work of Layamon was written during the first half of the thirteenth century. The language is that of the Southern dialect, and it represents the commencement of a new period, during which, after a violent struggle, in which the old inflections maintained their place side by side with the new, certain forms acquire the ascendency, to the exclusion of the others, and we consequently discover a greater simplicity of structure, and a more uniform employment of inflections than in works of the preceding period. "The language of Layamon," says Sir Frederick Madden, "belongs to that transition period, in which the groundwork of Anglo-Saxon phraseology still existed, although gradually yielding to the influence of the popular forms of speech." We find in it marked indications of a tendency to adopt those terminations and sounds which characterize a language in a state of change, and which are apparent in some other branches of the Teutonic tongue. As illustrating the "progress made in two centuries in departing from the ancient and purer grammatical forms, as found in Anglo-Saxon manuscripts, he mentions the use of *a* as an article, the change of the Anglo-Saxon terminations *a* and *an*, into *e* and *en*, as well as the disregard of inflections and genders, the masculine forms given to neuter nouns in the plural, the neglect of the feminine terminations of adjectives and pronouns, and confusion between the definite and indefinite declensions, the introduction of the preposition *to* before infinitives, and occasional use of weak preterites of verbs and participles instead of strong, the constant occurrence of *en* for *on* in the plural of verbs, and frequent elision of the final *e*, together with uncertainty in the rule for the government of prepositions." In the earlier text one of the most striking peculiarities is what Sir Frederick Madden has termed the "*nunnation*," consisting of the addition of a final *n* to certain cases of nouns and adjectives, to some tenses of verbs, and to several other parts of speech. One fact deserving particular attention in the English of Layamon, is the very slight infusion of Norman-French or Latin words. In the earlier text* we do not find more than fifty French words (even including some that may have come directly from the Latin), and of these fifty, several were in use in the preceding century. The later text retains about thirty of these, and adds about forty new ones, so that "if we reckon ninety words of French origin in both texts, containing together more than fifty-six thousand eight hundred, we shall be able to form a tolerably correct estimate of how little the English language was affected by foreign converse, even as late as the middle of the thirteenth century." Layamon's poem contains about thirty-two thousand two hundred and fifty lines, and the additions to the original constitute the finest portions of the work. "The structure of Layamon's poem," says Sir Frederick Madden, "consists

---

* There are two texts of Layamon's "Brut" in existence, the first of which was probably written about 1200; the second about 1250.

partly of lines in which the alliterative system of the Anglo-Saxons is preserved, and partly of couplets of unequal length, rhyming together." Many couplets occur in which all these forms are intermingled, while in others they are not found at all, and the two systems are used in so arbitrary a manner, the author passing from rhyme to alliteration, and from alliteration to rhyme, that it is almost impossible to ascertain the relative proportions of each. Upon the whole the alliterative portion greatly predominates over the rhymes, even including the assonant rhymes, or those in which the vowels agree while the consonants are different, which is of frequent occurrence, though almost unknown elsewhere in English poetry.*

The "Ancren Riwle," or "Anchorites' Rule," possesses little literary interest, though it is of decided philological or grammatical importance. It is a code of monastic regulations or precepts, written probably by an ecclesiastic, for the guidance of three ladies to whom it is addressed, and who formed a religious association, at Tarente, in Dorsetshire. The work was probably written late in the twelfth century, if not early in the thirteenth, and is therefore almost contemporaneous with the Chronicle of Layamon, to the earlier text of which it exhibits a striking likeness.

The literary merit of the work does not entitle it to

---

* "One of the most remarkable orthographical changes in the work of Layamon, is the change from initial *hw* to *wh*; compare *hwo*, who, *hwich*, *which*. This transposition was not regularly employed by any writer before Layamon. Another noteworthy feature is his regular and accurate employment of shall and will as auxiliaries."—*Marsh*. " Layamon is the last writer who retains an echo of the literary Anglo-Saxon."—*Earle*.

especial attention, and it is merely on account of its value as illustrating the progress of transition from Saxon to English, that we include it in our history of the language. "The spelling," says Mr. Morton, "whether from carelessness or want of system, is of an uncommon and unsettled character, and may be pronounced barbarous and uncouth. The language is semi-Saxon, or Anglo-Saxon somewhat changed, and in the first of the various stages through which it had to pass, before it arrived at the copiousness and elegance of our modern English. The inflections, which originally marked the oblique cases of substantive nouns, and also the distinctions of gender, are for the most part discarded. Yet as these changes are partial and incomplete, enough of the more ancient characteristics of the language is left to justify the inference that the innovations are recent. Not only is *es* of the genitive case retained, but we very often meet with the dative and accusative in *e*, and the accusative in *en*, as *then, the*. We meet also occasionally with the genitive in *re* from the Saxon *ra*, and *ne* and *ene* from *ena*. The cases and genders of adjectives are generally disused, but not always. The moods and tenses of the verbs are little altered from the older forms, and in many words they are not changed at all. The infinitive, which in pure Saxon ends invariably in *an*, is changed into *en*." From the general character of its structure, and from its resemblance to the older text of Layamon, Mr. Morton concludes that in the "Ancren Riwle" we have a specimen of the language of the West of England in the thirteenth century. One essential difference between the "Brut" of Layamon and the "Ancren Riwle," is the much greater proportion of French words contained in the latter work. This, however, may be readily explained, as the topics discussed in the "Ancren Riwle" are theological and moral, and consequently required the employment of a Latin and French vocabulary.

The "Ormulum" (1215) is described by its editor, Dr. White, as "a series of homilies in an imperfect state, composed in metre without alliteration, and, except in very few cases, also without rhyme; the subject of the homilies being supplied by those portions of the New Testament which were read in the daily service of the church, the design of the writer being, first to give a paraphrastic version of the Gospel of the day, adapting the matter to the rules of his verse, with such verbal additions as were required for that purpose." The "Ormulum" (so called from its author, Orm, a monk of the Augustine Order) has more interest, both in a literary and philological point of view, than any other work of the Transition Period. Orm appears to have been an orthoëpist of nature's own making, and in his ingeniously devised system of spelling, we have the first known attempt at orthoëpical reform in the history of our tongue. The assiduous and painstaking labors of the author, and his quaint devices for indicating the sounds of words by technical contrivances, imply a conscious appreciation of the anomalies and diversities of English spelling, and his praiseworthy efforts were probably designed to establish, or at least to preserve, a standard of correct pronunciation in the midst of dialectic divergences and confusions. The principal peculiarities of Orm's orthography consist "in a doubling of the consonant whenever it follows a vowel having any sound except that which is now indicated by the annexation of a final *e* to the single consonant. Thus, *pane* would be written *pan* by Orm, but *pan, pann ; mean, men,* but *men, menn ; pine, pin,* but *pin, pinn ; tune, tun,* but *tun, tunn.*" The versification departs from the Anglo-Saxon standard, in wanting alliteration and in possessing a regular metrical flow; and from the Norman-French in wanting rhyme. The vocabulary is slightly affected by Latin elements, and scarcely at all by Norman-French influence. The structure of the "Ormulum" exhibits a more advanced stage of the language than Layamon; in fact, so regular is its syntax compared with that of contemporaneous compositions, that it might almost be styled English instead of Anglo-Saxon.

The "Chronicle of Robert of Gloucester" is a narrative of British and English history, from the siege of Troy to the death of Henry III., 1272. The earlier part of the work is founded upon Geoffrey of Monmouth's Latin History, but it is destitute of skill or imagination. "The author," says Warton, "has clothed the fables of Geoffrey of Monmouth in rhyme, which have often a more poetical air in Geoffrey's prose." The "Chronicle," however, is worthy of notice, not only on account of its contributions to our knowledge of the history of England in the thirteenth century, but also because it is the oldest professed historical composition in the language. The style is that of the Western English. To the student of English philology, the work is peculiarly interesting, as illustrating the state of the language about the accession of Edward I., and also for the information it conveys respecting the bilingual condition of England produced by the introduction of the Norman tongue, and its prevalence during the author's lifetime, more than two centuries after the Conquest. We transcribe the following lines :

Thus come lo! Engelonde into Normannes honde,
And the Normans ne couthe speke tho bote her owe speche,
And speke French as dude atom, and here chyldren dude also teche,
So that heymen of thys lond, that of her blod come,
Holdeth alle thulke speche that hii of hem none
Vor bote a man couthe French, me tolth of hym well lute,
Ac lowe men holdeth to Englyss, and to her kunde speche yute,
Ich wene ther be ne man in world countreyes none,
That ne holdeth to her kunde speche, but Engelond one,
Ac wel me wot vor to conne bothe wel yt ys,
Vor the more that a man con, the more worth he ys.

That is: Thus lo! England came into the hand of the Normans, and the Normans could not speak then but their own speech, and spoke French, as they did at home, and their children did all so teach; so that high men of this land that of their blood come, retain all the same speech that they of them took. For unless a man know French, one talketh of him little. But low men hold to English and to their natural speech yet. I imagine there be no people in any country of the world that do not hold to their natural speech but in England alone. But well I wot it is well for to know both, for the more that a man knows the more worth he is.

CHAPTER VI.

THE RISE OF THE ENGLISH LANGUAGE.

The works of the Transition era enable us to trace with tolerable accuracy the series of changes by which Anglo-Saxon passed from its inflected to its uninflected stage. So gradual and difficult of chronological determination are the changes which occur in every tongue, that it is impossible to fix with precision a point at which a language may be said to pass from one phase into another, from its radical to its agglutinative stage, or from its agglutinative to its inflected form. All such determinations of the periods of a language are to a certain extent arbitrary, and the most that can be accomplished is to approximate with some degree of correctness to those almost impalpable boundaries at which one speech fades into another, or passes from the exuberant vigour of youth to the maturity of manhood, or from the maturity of manhood to the infirmity of age.

By the middle, or *about* the middle, of the thirteenth century, the Anglo-Saxon dialects had undergone so marked a simplification of structure that we are enabled to discover a gradual approximation to their modern representative, the standard English of the present day. The rise of the English tongue, as a new form of speech, may thus be dated from about the middle of the thirteenth century, A. D. 1250. But this must be carefully distinguished from the rise of the Queen's English, or literary form of the language, which did not acquire the ascendency until a later period. There was at this period no generally received standard of speech. English had commenced its history, but it consisted merely of a congeries of dialects, which had diverged from the Anglo-Saxon stem, each having its grammatical peculiarities and its literature, however imperfect; varying in different localities, and agreeing only in one essential particular, the loss of inflections and general simplification of structure.

Between the years 1215 and 1350, we trace the vigourous and praiseworthy efforts of the Saxon writers to establish a national literature. The poems of "Genesis and Exodus," "Havelok the Dane," the "Owl and the Nightingale," the "Romance of King Alexander," the "Chronicle of Robert of Gloucester," may be mentioned as exemplifications of this tendency.* But these productions, although enduring memorials of the patriotism of their authors, serve to illustrate the divided and dialectic condition of the language from the twelfth to the fourteenth century. During this long era of depression, Norman-French retained the ascendency as the dialect of the court and of fashionable circles, from which the verses of the Saxon poets were rigourously excluded. From the Conquest to about the middle of the fourteenth century, all the fashionable or popular literature of Eng-

---

* By many philologists and critics, the celebrated "Proclamation of Henry III." (1258) is considered the first specimen of composition in the English tongue. But it bears no resemblance to the literary English, as has been pointed out by Mr. Earle. The proclamation has been printed from the original document, by Mr. Ellis, and it may be found among the publications of the Early English Text Society; also in Earle's "Philology of the English Tongue," and in Corson's "Hand-Book of Anglo-Saxon and Early English."

land was written in the Norman tongue. It was the language of light literature, of the romances, the ballads, and metrical chronicles, designed to entertain the Norman nobility and their followers. Their merits must have been of an inferior order, if we may judge from the ridicule with which they were assailed by Chaucer. The great mass of Norman-French literature was produced in England; its cultivation commenced in that land, the Normans having no literature worthy of mention at the era of the Conquest. The fact to be particularly noted in this connection is, that during this long interval of gloom and oppression, from Aelfric to Chaucer, the vernacular tongue never ceased to be cultivated. Expelled from elegant and courtly association, dissevered into dialects, unable to compete with the dominant idiom, it was cherished with assiduous diligence in the monasteries and abbeys, and many of the literary memorials of this age are remarkable compositions, if we consider the circumstances under which they were produced.

But this protracted period of national and linguistic depression was to be relieved by the coming of a brighter day. Hitherto we have seen merely a discordant English language, without generally acknowledged standards or canons of literature. There was no national speech and no national unity until the middle of the fourteenth century. The Anglo-Saxon as the language of the people, the Latin as the dialect of learning and the clergy, and the French as the speech of the court and the aristocracy, existed side by side, without seriously affecting or modifying each other's vocabulary until about the reign of Edward III., 1327–77.

The distrust and animosity generated by the Conquest prevented a blending either of nationalities or dialects, and the two languages, like the two races, pursued their courses like parallel streams, without converging or commingling. The Norman-French dislocated the inflections of English, and disturbed its pronunciation; while Anglo-Saxon imparted a number of words to the vocabulary of French. To all intents, however, the two tongues remained essentially separate, and each imparted as much as it received. But those important political events that clouded the latter years of Edward's brilliant reign, the loss of all the splendid Continental acquisitions of England (which embraced the Atlantic coast of France, and which were further advanced, both in social and intellectual culture than the Normans of England), marked the commencement of a new era in the history of the English race and the English tongue. The disasters which cast a shadow over the declining years of this glorious reign, led to the renunciation of those cherished dreams of foreign conquest that had captivated the imagination and fired the knightly spirit of Englishmen, and tended powerfully to blend into a homogeneous mass the discordant populations of the island, to make England the centre of their affections and their interests—their common country. "Had the Plantagenets," says Macaulay, "as at one time seemed likely, succeeded in uniting all France under their government, it is probable that England would never have had an independent existence. The noble language of Milton and Burke would have remained a rustic dialect, without a literature, a fixed grammar, or a fixed orthography, and would have been contemptuously abandoned to the boors. No man of English extraction would have risen to eminence, except by becoming in speech and in habits a Frenchman." Whatever sentimental regrets we may be disposed to indulge for the loss of the magnificent conquests of Edward III., and the Black Prince, yet it is at this epoch that we must date the commencement of English greatness. The energies of her people, diverted from the thoughts of Continental empire, were now directed to the development of a country which was henceforth to be the seat of their power; and from this era, the English tongue, partaking of the spirit and the aspirations of those who spoke it, woke from its long lethargy, and entered upon its unparalleled career. Under the influence of these important political events, social jealousies and national hostilities began slowly to fade away, as the two languages and the two races began gradually to melt into one.* Unity and harmony of sentiment, the partial concession of political privileges to the humbler classes, the formation of social alliance among the hitherto isolated nationalities, necessarily led to the partial blending of the two idioms, and to their reciprocal action and influence. For nearly two hundred years after the Conquest, English appears to have been spoken and written without any serious admixture of French. "The entire English vocabulary of the thirteenth century, so far as it is known to us in its printed literature, consists of about eight thousand words. Of these about one thousand, or between twelve and thirteen per cent., are of Latin or Romance origin,"† a striking illustration of the slight impression that the long continuance of French domination in England had made upon the vocabulary of the vernacular tongue. It was

---

* The union of the two races had been *partially* accomplished in the reign of Henry II., and in the reign of John, by the conquest of Normandy (1204), and by the enactment of Magna Charta (1215).

† Marsh's "Origin and History of the English Language."

the structure of the language that principally suffered from foreign contact, during the two centuries following the Conquest. Nor did the Norman-French escape the pernicious effects of foreign influence. On the contrary, it experienced decided alterations from its contact with the decaying Saxon, and suffered as much mutation as it had produced. Upon the conquest of Normandy from King John in 1204 by Philip Augustus, the kings of England ceased to be dukes of Normandy, and the Norman language, separated from the culture of its ancestral home, gradually declined in purity; it lost its original accentuation, and assumed an insular character. It acquired an antiquated and incorrect air; certain features belonging to the provincial dialect of Normandy had engrafted themselves upon it, and its pronunciation seems to have resembled the accent of Lower Normandy. In addition, this accent, when introduced into England, received a perceptible impress from Saxon articulation. The speech of the Anglo-Norman barons was distinguished from that of Normandy by a stronger articulation of particular syllables, and more especially of the final consonants. It was corrupted by Anglicisms, and was sometimes little more than a mutilated English. Even persons of culture, like Chaucer's gentle and decorous Prioress, spoke a French which was utterly opposed "to French of Paris," for although she could speak it "ful fayre and fetisly," she followed the French of "Stratford atte Bowe, for Frenche of Paris was to hire (her) unknowe."

If such was the French of the educated, we can readily imagine what it must have been in the mouths of the peasantry who affected to understand it. Trevisa tells us, "Jack wold be a gentleman yf he coude speke Frensche."

"In Piers Ploughman," says Mr. Earle, "we have the dykers and delvers, with their bits of French, doing a very bad day's work, but eminently polite to the ladies of the family:

'Dykers and Delvers that don here werk ille,
And driveth forth the longe day, with Deu, vous saue, dam emme.'"

These specimens will illustrate the extended prevalence of French in England, as well as its deformed and debased condition. The more widely it was diffused, the less firm was its sway, until in the fourteenth century it was a general subject of jest and ridicule. But as the French declined, the native language was growing more and more into repute. The new political and social conditions of which we have spoken, were beginning to accomplish their natural result. The commingling of the two races involved a coalescence of the two tongues. Henceforth the native language began to adopt and naturalize French vocables, appropriating them, not as badges of subjection, but as trophies of a successful contest against a valiant and determined foe. The adoption and intermixture of French words commenced when English was received as the speech of that part of the nation which had previously spoken French. So rapidly did the language, now conscious of its powers, and anticipating the brilliant triumphs in reserve for it, absorb the foreign material, that between 1300 and 1350, as many Latin and French words were introduced into the vocabulary of the English tongue, as in the whole period of more than two centuries that had intervened between the Conquest and the commencement of the fourteenth century. About the middle of this century, the native speech appears in full vigour and promise; the era of its gloom and depression is passed. Trevisa designates the great plague of 1349 as a point after which the popular fancy for speaking French began to abate. He says: "This was moche used tofore the grete deth, but sith it is somedele chaunged. For John Cornwaile, a maister of gramar, chaungide the lore (learning) in gramar scole and construction of (from) Frensch into Englisch, and Richard Pencriche lerned that maner teching of him, and other men of Pencriche. So that now, the yere of owre Lord, a thousand thre hundred four score and fyve (1349), of the secunde King Rychard after the Conquest nyne, in alle the gramar scoles of England, children leveth Frensch; and construeth and lerneth an (in) Englisch."

In 1362 was passed the statute enacting that all pleas pleaded in the King's Courts should be pleaded in the English tongue, and enrolled in Latin; the pleadings previously to this time having been entered in French, and the enrollments of them sometimes in French, and sometimes in Latin. Thus we see the English language restored to its natural rights in the schools of the realm, and in the courts of law. The reason alleged for the last-mentioned change was, that the French language had become so much unknown in the realm, that the people who were parties to suits at law had no knowledge nor understanding of that which is said for or against them by their sergeants and other pleaders. Yet, strangely enough, this very statute is in French, which, though it had ceased to be the language of the people, continued to a considerably later period to be the mother tongue of the Norman dynasty, and probably that generally spoken at Court, and in the House of Lords.

Edward III. wrote his letters and despatches in French, and there is but one recorded instance in which this monarch is known to have used the English tongue.

It was during the first half of the fifteenth century that the English language, growing more and more into repute, ended by totally supplanting the French, except with the great barons, who, before they renounced the dialect of their fatherland, beguiled their weary hours with works in both languages. Towards the end of the fifteenth century, the kings of England and their courtiers appear to have spoken the French with fluency and correctness; but this was purely an individual accomplishment. The Norman was no longer the vernacular speech of the great, nor the idiom with which children were acquainted from their cradles; it was cultivated merely as an intellectual discipline or a polite accomplishment, as in the present age we study the languages of Greece and Rome.

Thus, about four centuries after the battle of Hastings, disappear the differences of dialect, which, together with the disparity of social conditions, had marked the separation of the two races, the one descended from the followers of William, and the other from the followers of Harold.

CHAPTER VII.

THE RISE OF THE ENGLISH LANGUAGE (*continued*).

In the preceding chapter we endeavoured to indicate the causes, social and political, which blended the opposing Saxons and Normans, and restored the native language to its natural and inalienable privileges. By the action of those causes, there were gradually created a national speech and a national sentiment, but the fusion was not complete; the proportion of Norman and Saxon elements in the newly formed tongue was not definitely ascertained; it wanted that harmony, symmetry, and precision which are acquired only by judicious culture, and by the establishment of generally acknowledged standards of literary excellence. Hence, what the language needed, for the development of its powers, was the moulding influence of some great word artist, who could assign to the constituents of the vocabulary their rank and proportion, regulate its syntactical structure, and render it the fit medium for the loftiest sentiments, the grandest aspirations, that were to be embodied in it. It was not until the tongue had been transmuted by the plastic touch of Chaucer, had given utterance to the oracles of God, under the guidance of Wycliffe, and been refined by the precise and accurate rhyme of "ancient Gower," that it advanced to that pre-eminence which it has maintained above all the languages of Europe.

THE RISE OF THE ENGLISH LANGUAGE.   73

Let us first observe the process by which the vocabulary of the fourteenth century was formed, the sources whence its varied wealth was gathered, ere it was subjected to the delicate scrutiny of Chaucer, and was regulated by the precise and accurate rhyme of Gower.

It is a prevalent though a mistaken impression, that the great number of French words which flowed into the English language during the fourteenth century are to be attributed to poetry, and other departments of literature. "The law, which now first became organized into a science, introduced very many terms borrowed from the nomenclature of Latin and French jurisprudence; the glass-worker, the enameller, the architect, the brass-founder, the Flemish clothier, whom Norman taste and luxury invited, or domestic oppression expelled, from the Continent, brought with them the vocabularies of their respective arts; and Mediterranean commerce, which was stimulated by the demand for English wool, then the finest in Europe, imported from the harbours of a sea where French was the predominant language, both new articles of merchandise and the French designations of them. The sciences too, medicine, physics, geography, alchemy, astrology, all of which became known to England chiefly through French channels, added numerous specific terms to the existing vocabulary."[*] The poets, so far from marring the native speech by too copious an infusion of French words, were reserved in their employment of them, and when not compelled by the necessities of versification, selected a vocabulary principally composed of Anglo-Saxon words. The correctness of this assertion may be established by

---

[*] Marsh's "History of the English Language."

comparing the dialect of the prose writers of this era, with those poetical compositions which are designed for the least refined classes, and which, consequently, employ the simplest and most unpretending diction. This has been admirably illustrated by Mr. Marsh in his "Origin and History of the English Language," 268–270. Sir John Mandeville is the first regular prose writer who employed the newly formed language. After spending many years in foreign travel, he returned to England, and composed (1356) an account of his travels, written in Latin, translated into French, and then into English, "that every man of his nation might read and understand it." The book appears to have had a very extensive circulation, as there are many copies in existence, and its vocabulary must have been perfectly intelligible to the masses of English-speaking people. Though the style and syntactical structure of Mandeville are English, the proportion of Latin and French words employed in his unadorned, unpoetical narrative, is greater than is found in the works of Langlande, Chaucer, Gower, or any other English poet of the fourteenth century. In the prologue, which contains, exclusive of Latin and Greek proper names, less than twelve hundred words, more than one hundred and thirty, or eleven per cent., are of Latin or French origin, and of these, the following are new to English, not being found in the printed literature of the preceding century: Assembly, because, comprehend, conquer, certain, environ, excellent, former (noun), frailty, glorious, inflame, inumber (inumbrate), moisten, nation, people, philosopher, plainly, proclaim, promise, pronounce, province, publish, reconcile, redress, subject, temporal, translate, trespasser, visit. The following words contained in

Chapters I., II., III., XXI., XXII., were first pointed out by Mr. Marsh. Abstain, abundant, ambassador, anoint, apparel, appear, appraise, array, attendance; benefice, benignly, bestial; calculation, cause, chaplet, cherish, circumcision, claim, command (verb), comparison, continually, contrarious, contrary, convenient, convert, corner, cover, cruelty, cubit, curiously; date, defend (forbid), degree, deny, deprive, desert (waste), devoutly, diaper, discordant, discover, disfigured, dispend, dissever, diversity, duchy; enemy, enforce, engender, estate, estimation, examine; faithfully, fiercely, foundation, fornication; generation, governance, gum; idol, immortal, imprint, incline, inspiration; join; letters (alphabetic characters), lineage; marquis, menace, minstrelsy, money, monster, mortal, multitude; necessary; obedient, obeissante, obstacle, officer, opinion, ordinance, ordinately, orient, ostrich, outrageously; paper, pasture, pearls, perch (a pole), perfectly, profitable, promise (noun), proper (own), province, purple; quantity; rebellion, receive, region, relation, religious, return, reverend, royalty, royally, rudely; sacrament, science, search, scripture, servitor, signification, simony, soldier, solemn, specialty, spiritual, stranger, subjection, superscription; table, temporal, testament, throne (verb), tissue, title (inscription); unction, usury; value, vary, vaulted, vessel, vicar, victory, vulture.

We find, then, in the prologue, and in the five chapters from which these words are taken, comprising about one-eighth of the volume, one hundred and seventy-four words of Latin and Romance origin, not contained in the printed literature of the thirteenth century. It is evident, from the results of this investigation, that the charge so often preferred against the poets of the fourteenth century, of having corrupted the purity of their native tongue by foreign admixture, is unsupported and unjust. It was the serious diminution of its resources that the Anglo-Saxon had experienced during the dreary period of its literary subjection, when its powers were enfeebled for lack of assiduous culture, and its intellectual and moral vocabulary languished and decayed, which rendered necessary the introduction of Latin and French terms. We have already alluded to the richness of its theological and intellectual vocabulary, and it was in these departments that it had encountered the severest losses. So long as England remained independent of Continental alliances, the Saxon preserved its copious spiritual nomenclature, unaffected by foreign admixture or interference. The reign of Edward the Confessor introduced England into the sphere of Continental relations, and the Conquest gave the finishing stroke to the employment of Saxon for ecclesiastical and spiritual purposes; Norman priests and teachers adhered pertinaciously to the consecrated dialect of Rome, and the native spiritual and intellectual vocabulary, falling into disuse, became gradually obsolete. Hence, when the new language began to be employed as a literary speech, its defects in these essential particulars had to be remedied by calling into service the corresponding terms in the Norman tongue. The old and oft repeated complaint, urged against the poets of this century by Gil, Verstegan, and Skimer, is not sustained by the evidence; it was an erroneous opinion, based upon an imperfect acquaintance with the historical development of our language. The foreign vocables would doubtless have secured all the privileges of English citizenship, if the fourteenth century did not record the name of a single poet. The language was recovering its consciousness; a coalescence of the separated nationalities involved a blending of their tongues, and the influx of foreign words was a necessity, which, in any event, must have resulted from the altered political and social relations of the kingdom. It was the exalted function of the poets of this age to refine, polish, and skilfully dispose of the linguistic materials, that the fusion of races, and the other causes indicated above, had accumulated; to adjust the imperfectly blended elements, assigning to each its importance; and from their harmonious commingling, to evolve a language adequate to all the demands of the peerless literature that was to be treasured up in it. The poets, in short, were the arbiters, the umpires, the law-givers of the language.

CHAPTER VIII.

PIERS, THE PLOWMAN.

The interest and importance of "The Vision of Piers Plowman" arise not so much from its literary execution, or its intrinsic excellence, as from the fact that it is the first composition in which the English spirit and genius are distinctly perceptible. The history of English literature dates from the age of Chaucer and Gower, under whose guidance the literary speech assumed a definite form and character. But the "Vision of the Plowman," though written in a dialect, presaged the speedy advent of that glorious morn, when the new language and the new literature were to enter upon that magnificent career which have made them the wonder of our history. Piers Plowman, then, is the first writer, truly English in sentiment, and his "Vision" is an appropriate prelude to those grand bursts of melody that were soon to fill the balmy air with "sounds that echo still."

It is difficult to ascertain with precision the date of the poem known as "The Vision of Piers Plowman," but it was probably composed about 1360–70. The authorship of the work is also involved in obscurity, and the tradition which ascribes it to Robert Langlande, an English ecclesiastic, is not established by trustworthy evidence. But a fictitious Langlande has long had the credit of the poem, and as no conclusive testimony has been adduced to invalidate his claim, there is no danger of doing injustice to the genuine author, by appropriating the name of Langlande as the impersonation of some unknown writer. The acquaintance with ecclesiastical literature which the poem displays, indicates that the author was connected with the clerical profession. He foreshadowed the teachings of Wycliffe, and he perhaps ultimately attained the same conclusions as this illustrious champion of the truth. Every writer who secures an abiding-place in the memory of his countrymen must be, in a greater or less degree, an exponent of the age; he must embody and reflect its intellectual sentiments and tendencies, its religious and political opinions. In the dawn of every literature this principle forms an essential element of success, and the author of the "Vision" merely invested with poetic garb the sympathies and the aspirings in which every English heart participated. The "Vision of Piers Plowman," therefore, derives its poetic interest, not from its revelation of unknown truths, but from its lucid reflection of the life and character of the age, its exposure of ecclesiastical corruptions, its distinctive dialect and alliterative form, which gave it an extensive circulation among the humbler classes. It bodied forth those grand religious dogmas which were dimly apprehended, and by presenting them forcibly to the consciousness of the English people, it prepared the way for the reception of those tenets which the efforts of Wycliffe and his adherents were already disseminating. The numerous manuscripts of the work in existence, show how general its circulation must have been, and the marked variations in different copies prove that it was deemed worthy of diligent recension by the original author, or, at least, that it was essentially modified by the scribes to whose inspection it had been submitted. The "Vision" had become a national possession, a sort of "didactic catechism." The querulous tone which pervades the work would tend to increase its popularity among the middle classes, who, though gradually acquiring a degree of social and political influence, were not yet sufficiently powerful to protect themselves against the encroachments of their civil and ecclesiastical rulers. One circumstance that invests the poem with peculiar interest, is its adherence to the ancient alliterative system of versification; and it was the last work of eminence that conformed to the canons of Anglo-Saxon verse. The "Vision of the Plowman" displays the accurate acquaintance of its author with the Latin Scriptures, the treatises of the Fathers, and the works of Romish expositors, though it contains few indications of a knowledge of Romance literature. Still, the proportion of Norman-French words, or at least of Norman-French words assimilated to Latin, is equal to that contained in the poetry of Chaucer. While the conception of the poem was doubtless induced by the moral and political condition of contemporary England, the manner of treatment is purely original; its whole tenor is an entire departure from the established character of Anglo-Saxon poetry. Though the poem is defective in unity of plan, its intent and spirit are one. The scope of the poem is restricted, being to a considerable extent in the form of a dialogue. In these portions, the language represents the dialect of common life, though the characters are not delineated with sufficient individuality to invest it with a dramatic colouring. It was, however, well adapted to the intelligence of the class for whom it was designed, as is attested by its extended circulation, notwithstanding its occasional introduction of Latin quotations.

The diction of the "Vision" is more archaic than that of Chaucer; many of its words have become obsolete, and some have entirely disappeared. The syntax, the structure, and the vocabulary, however, present as marked a resemblance as those of any two modern authors who should discuss topics so unrelated, and address audiences so diverse, as the cavaliers of Chaucer and the peasants of Langlande.* The following outline will illustrate the grammar of Piers the Plowman.

Nouns. The nominative plural commonly ends in *es*, as in *shroudes;* sometimes in s, as *bidders;* or in z, as in *diamantz*. For *es*, *is* is sometimes found, as in *wittis*, and very rarely *us*, as *folus;* some few plurals are in *en*, as *chylderen*. A few nouns, such as *folk*, which were originally neuter, have no termination in the plural. *Gees, men*, are plurals formed by vowel change; *fete* and feet are various spellings of the plural of foot.

Cases. The genitive singular ends in *es*, sometimes corrupted into *is*, as *cattes, cattis;* other endings are very rare. The genitive plural ends in *en* or *ene*, as *clerken*. The dative singular commonly ends in *e*, as in *to bedde*.

Adjectives. The distinction between definite and indefinite adjectives is difficult, owing to the irregularity of the alliterative rhythm, and the additions of copyists and scribes. Plural adjectives should end in *e*, and generally do, as *alle*. The re-duplication of a consonant when a syllable is added is worth notice; thus *alle* is the plural

---

* Langlande wrote in the dialect of the Western shires, but his style is marked by Midland peculiarities.

of *al*, as *shullen* is the plural of the auxiliary *shal*. Very rarely plural adjectives of French origin end in *es*. The comparative of *heigh* is *herre;* superlative, *hexte*. Adjectives and adverbs ending in *ly*, sometimes form their comparatives and superlatives in *loker, lokest*, as *light, lightloker, lightlokest*.

Pronouns are the same as in Chaucer, but besides *sche*, the older form *heo* is used, and besides *pei*, the older form *h* (hy). There are also traces of dialectic confusion and admixture in the use of the pronouns; *their* is denoted by *here, her,* or *hri;* *them* by *hem*, etc., etc.

Verbs. The indicative plural ends both in *en* and *eth*, as *geten, conneth*. The past tense of weak verbs which should end in *ede*, ends, commonly, in *ed* only, both in the singular and plural, as *pley-ed*, but sometimes the full plural form, -*eden* occurs. In weak verbs, which should form their past tenses in *de* or *te*, the final *e* is often dropped. Thus, *went* for *wente*. In strong verbs, which should terminate (in the first and third persons singular of the past tense) in a consonant, we often find an *e* added; thus: *I shope* for *I shop*. The plural generally has the correct form, *en*, as *chosen*. In the infinitive mood some verbs are found with the ending *ie* or *ye*, and final *e* is sometimes dropped. The present participle ends in *yng*, as *worchyng;* the prefix *y* is often found before past participles, sometimes even before past tenses.*

The words are selected with care, and employed with discrimination as well as with reference to their radical significance. Notwithstanding the allegorical drapery of the "Vision," it affords us a graphic portraiture of

---

* Skeat's Introduction to "Piers Plowman."

English society in the fourteenth century; it removes the obscuring veil, and allows us a glimpse of the inner life of the nation.—We have incidental descriptions of the food, the dress, the domestic status of the humbler classes, the foul dealing of tradesmen and mechanics; in short, a vivid portraiture of English life in the fourteenth century, drawn by a contemporary, and surpassing in naturalness the intricate details of the historian. Though the poem does not enter into chronological discussion, it is a valuable addition to our knowledge of English character and English society in the age that produced a Chaucer and a Wycliffe.

CHAPTER IX.

THE WYCLIFFITE VERSIONS OF THE SCRIPTURES.

The Wycliffite versions of the Scriptures exerted a decided influence in developing that particular dialect of English which became the literary form of the language. They thus tended to prepare the way for Chaucer and Gower, the former of whom was probably indebted to the Wycliffite translations for much of the wealth and beauty of his diction and vocabulary. The Wycliffite versions of the Scriptures are therefore entitled to special consideration in a history which treats of the origin and formation of the English tongue. Though the Anglo-Saxon possessed a native translation of the Gospels, and of some other portions of the Bible, there is no reason to suppose that any considerable part of the Scriptures, except the Psalter, had been rendered into English until the translation of the entire sacred volume was attempted, by the advice of Wycliffe, and partially executed by him about the last quarter of the fourteenth century. Whatever Biblical knowledge the English had acquired was gathered from their clergy, who introduced into their discourses translations from the Vulgate, or Latin version of St. Jerome. These were not intended for circulation, and consequently no opportunity was afforded for the study of the Scriptures in the vernacular tongue. The translation of Wycliffe was made from the Latin Vulgate, the authorized version of the Romish Church. There is no direct evidence to prove that any of the translators were sufficiently versed in the Greek and Hebrew to translate directly from either of those tongues, and, in consequence, the structural peculiarities, or the phraseological combinations, which they impressed upon their version, are derived from the Vulgate, except so far as the style and diction of the Vulgate itself had been affected by the syntax and vocabulary of the Greek and Hebrew.

No detailed examination of these works is contemplated, nor an endeavour to ascertain the share which Wycliffe had in the execution of them. It is sufficient for our purpose to say, that in the only trustworthy edition we have of any of them, the older text, from Genesis to Baruch, third chapter, twentieth verse, is probably the work of Hereford, an English ecclesiastic, while the remainder of the Old Testament, and the Apocrypha, are supposed to have been executed by Wycliffe. There exists no reasonable doubt that the whole New Testament was rendered into English by him. It is impossible to ascertain precisely the date of the commencement and completion of this important work, but there are good reasons for believing that the older text was finished about 1380, the revised edition of Purvey about 1390. Notwithstanding the labour and expense of transcribing, the translations appear to have been widely circulated, as many manuscripts are in existence.

The fidelity and accuracy that characterize the Wycliffe versions may be ascribed principally to the action of two causes: First, the translators, as well as the people, were imbued with those intense religious sensibilities, and that consciousness of intellectual elevation, which result from spiritual emancipation. Second, the structure of the language was then marked by simplicity and freedom of expression. Its elasticity and pliancy had not been checked by the imposition of grammatical canons or by the constraining influence of arbitrary prescription, and it therefore more closely conformed to the style of the original Scriptures than the polished and formal diction of later ages. These versions, consequently, display, in structure and in vocabulary, a closer assimilation to the spirit and genius of the ancient text than could have been attained with a fixed syntactical order and a vocabulary, a great proportion of whose words had assumed determinate and invariable shades of meaning. The most important result accomplished by these versions was the formation of an English religious dialect, which, with unessential modifications, has remained the language of devotion and of Scriptural translation to the present day. While our secular dialect has been fluctuating, inconsistent, and subject to frequent mutations, we have possessed from the dawn of our literary language a sacred vocabulary, idiomatic, uniform, and harmonious.

It is remarkable that the style of the original works supposed to have been written by Wycliffe, is much less regular than that of the New Testament, which, instead of exhibiting that discordance of forms characteristic of the authors of that period, appears to have adopted some model, and to have adhered to it without variation. The consistent and regular structure of Wycliffe's New Testament imparted to the work a pre-eminence as a standard of sacred and devotional phraseology, and many of the archaic constructions of the Authorized Version, as well as many of its special forms, were transferred by Purvey and Tyndale from Wycliffe, and from Tyndale by the translators of King James's reign, remaining unchanged during a period of five centuries. To so great an extent are the Wycliffite versions the basis of all succeeding translations, that though the reader may occasionally be perplexed by an obsolete word, an archaic idiom, or an antique spelling, it is plausibly conjectured by an eminent critic, that if the illustrious Reformer were restored to life he would be able to read and understand our modern edition of the Bible without assistance. The writings of Langlande and of Wycliffe (particularly the latter) introduced into the English language a great number of words derived directly from the Latin, or from the Latin through the Norman-French. They conferred a more important benefit upon the colloquial dialect by giving a general circulation to many Latin and French words which had never acquired popular acceptance, but had been restricted to literary use. The dissemination of "Piers the Plowman's Vision" among the higher classes was prevented by its retention of the ancient alliterative versification, and the works of Wycliffe were, in a great measure, banished from the same circles by the conjoint action of the secular and spiritual power, as seditious and heretical. Hence, their circulation was confined to that class whose obscurity afforded them immunity from civil and ecclesiastical persecution. Notwithstanding these unfavourable surroundings, the translators of the fourteenth century and their polemical compositions perceptibly increased the richness of our moral and theological vocabulary, and much of the excellence of our present version of the Scriptures is due to the valuable accessions which our language received from their assiduous labours. While the writings of Wycliffe cannot be regarded as models of the literary language as it existed in his age, they contributed efficaciously by their excellence and their extensive circulation to the importance of the East Midland dialect, and thus tended essentially to secure for that speech the pre-eminence as the standard form of the language. It is probable, too, that they contributed to the verbal affluence of Chaucer, and in this manner exerted a specific influence in enriching the vocabulary of the new-born tongue. The political faction with which Chaucer sympathized was disposed to regard the Reformer with favour, and must have cherished a kindly sentiment towards the common people, who formed the reading public of Langlande and Wycliffe. Hence we may readily imagine that Chaucer had perused the translation of the Scriptures as well as the "Vision of the Plowman;" nor could a genius of his subtle perception fail to discover that these works treasured up verbal gems of purest ray, though in a crude and unpolished condition. These rich jewels, transmuted by his masterly touch, tended to enrich and gild his diction, and the surpassing excellence of his style is partly to be attributed to his skillful extraction of the pure gold from the writings of his contemporaries, a means of improvement to which the intolerance of inferior artists would not permit them to descend.

CHAPTER X.

THE ENGLISH LANGUAGE IN THE AGE OF CHAUCER.

In the preceding chapters, we endeavoured to indicate that series of processes by which the Anglo-Saxon tongue was divested of its synthetic form, and, deprived of the conservative power of literary nurture, gradually became disintegrated, diverging into several dialects, distinguished by well-defined grammatical and structural peculiarities. The language and the literature that we have hitherto considered are dialectic in character, as there was thus far no generally recognized standard of speech, and consequently no national literature. The commencement of literary English must be dated from the latter half of the fourteenth century, and from the writings of Chaucer and his contemporary, Gower. These are the true founders of the literary form of our tongue. Having arrived at this important point, the rise of the King's English, it may be well, before proceeding further, to notice minutely the precise condition which the language had attained at this period.

For the sake of method, it will be convenient to go through the several parts of speech in the order in which they are commonly ranged by grammarians.

First. The prepositive article, *re, reo, paet* (which answered to the ὁ ἡ τὸ of the Greeks), in all its varieties of gender, case, and number, had been long laid aside, and instead of it an indeclinable *the* was prefixed to all sorts of nouns, in all cases and in both numbers.

Second. The declensions of the nouns substantive were reduced from six to one, and instead of a variety of cases in both numbers, they had only a genitive case singular, which was uniformly deduced from the nominative by adding to it *es*; or only *s* if it ended in an *e* feminine; and that same form was used to express the plural number in all its cases. The nouns adjective had lost all distinction of gender, case, or number.

Third. The personal pronouns retained only one oblique case in each number. Their possessive pronouns were in the same condition with the adjectives. The interrogative and relative *who* had now only a genitive *whos*, and an accusative *whom*, and no variety of number. The demonstrative *this* and *that* had only the plurals *thise* and *tho*, and no case. Other pronominal words had become undeclined, with very few exceptions.

Fourth. The verbs were very nearly reduced to their present simple state, having four moods, the indicative, subjunctive, imperative, and infinitive, and two tenses, the present and the past. All the other varieties of mood and tense were expressed by auxiliary verbs. The future, with *shall*, was coming into use. It first occurs in Layamon, but the original meaning was retained by Chaucer: "For by the faithe I *schal (owe)* to God." The inflection of the verb in the singular number was nearly the same as at present, *I love, thou lovest, he loveth*. In the plural varying forms were used; sometimes the Saxon form in *eth* was used—*we, ye, they loveth;* sometimes the form in *en*—*we, ye, they loven*. This latter was the prevailing form in the past tense, plural number,—*we loveden*. The Saxon termination of the infinitive *an*, was changed to *en*—*to love* was gradually disappearing, leaving *to love*. The present participle generally ended in *ing*, but the ancient form in *ende* or *ande* was still in use—*lovende, lovande*. The progressive changes were *end, ind, in, ing*. The past participle was formed in *ed* or contractions of *ed*, such as *e* final, as *caste, hurte*. The past participle was also formed in *en*, particularly in irregular verbs. Sometimes the *n* was lost—*take* for *taken*. The auxiliaries were still inflected, though not long after Chaucer—*we shallen love*. *To have* and *to ben* were complete verbs, and the latter, with the past participle and the other auxiliary verbs, supplied the place of the passive voice.

Fifth. With respect to the indeclinable parts of speech, it is sufficient to remark that many of them remained pure Saxon; the greater number, however, were becoming abbreviated.

Such was the general condition of the Saxon element in the English language at the time that Chaucer commenced his literary career; let us notice briefly the accessions which it received at different periods from Normandy.

As the language of the Anglo-Saxons was complete in every essential respect, and had sufficed for the purposes of literary composition of diverse kinds, as well as for all the necessities of society, long before they had sustained any intimate relation to their Norman neighbours, there existed no inducement to alter its original and radical character, or even to deviate from its established forms. Consequently (as has just been pointed out), in all the essential parts of speech, the distinctive peculiarities of the Saxon idiom were retained without exception, while the numbers of French words that from time to time were introduced were assimilated either immediately or gradually to the Saxon idiom.

Sixth. The words thus introduced were principally nouns substantive, adjectives, verbs, and participles. The adverbs, which are derived from French adjectives, seem to have been formed from them after they were Anglicized, as they have all the Saxon termination *liche* or *ly*, instead of the French *ment*. As to the other indeclinable parts of speech, our language being sufficiently rich in its own resources, has borrowed nothing from France except an interjection or two. The nouns substantive in the French language (as in all the Romance dialects) had dropped their case endings long before the period of which we are at present speaking, but such of them as were naturalized in England acquired a genitive case, according to the corrupted Saxon form. The *plural* number was also new modelled to the same form, if necessary; for in the nouns ending in *e* feminine (as the greater part of the French did), the two languages were already agreed. Nominative *flour*, genitive *floures*, plural *floures*. Nominative *dame*, genitive *dames*, plural *dames*. On the contrary, the adjectives, which in their native land had a distinction of gender and number, upon their naturalization in England seem generally to have lost both, and to have assumed the simple form of the English adjective, without case, gender, or number. The French verbs laid aside all their differences of conjugation; *accorder, souffrir, recevoir, descendre* were regularly changed into *accorden, suffren, receiven, descenden*. They brought with them only two tenses, the present and the past, nor did they retain any peculiarity of inflexion which could distinguish them from verbs of Saxon origin. The participle of the present time, in some verbs, appears to have preserved its French form, as *usant, suffisant.* The participle of the past time adopted almost universally the regular Saxon termination in *ed*, as *accorded, received, descended.* It even frequently assumed the prepositive particle ȝe (or y, as it was afterwards written), which, among the Saxons, was generally, though not peculiarly, prefixed to that participle.

Upon the whole it may be affirmed that at the time of which we are speaking, although the *structure* of our language was still Saxon, the *vocabulary* was to a considerable extent French. The Conquest (1066) introduced many novelties; the mechanical arts, the civil law, the sciences, geography, medicine, alchemy, astrology, all brought with them their respective nomenclatures derived from the French and Latin tongues. The poets, who generally have the principal share in moulding and refining a language, introduced a great number of words from France. As they were, for a long period, chiefly translators, this expedient saved them the trouble of seeking out the cognate terms in Saxon. The French words were descended from a polished language, and were much better adapted to metrical uses than the Saxon; the final syllables of the French chimed together with more frequent consonances, and its accentual system, which tended to place the stress of the voice upon the final syllable, was better adapted to rhyming verse.*

---

* Tyrwhitt's Introduction to Chaucer.

CHAPTER XI.

THE AGE OF CHAUCER AND GOWER.

In the preceding chapter we indicated the general condition of the language about the time of Chaucer and Gower. We must now consider that particular form of the language in which their works were composed. This, in consequence of their influence and popularity, as well as the excellence and the superiority of their poetry, acquired the preëminence as the standard of literature, and constituted the King's English, or literary form of the tongue. Henceforth the other dialects descend to mere patois, and all other English gradually becomes provincial.

The brilliant genius, the lofty social position of Chaucer, as well as his harmonious adjustment of the native and foreign element in the vocabulary, and his fine verbal discrimination, were principally instrumental in elevating the East Midland dialect to the ascendency. The fame of Gower rests principally upon the accuracy and precision of his rhyme and vocabulary, which contributed efficaciously to determine the form of the language. The greater part of his works was composed in French; in literary merit he was far inferior to his great contemporary, nor does he appear to have written in English until encouraged by his example. The language which Chaucer adopted, and which by his influence became the standard form of the speech, was the East Midland dialect, in which Orm and Robert of Brunne had also written. This dialect, formed by the blending of Anglian and Danish terms and constructions, had gradually extended further and further southward, until it supplanted the original Southern speech, which had steadily receded before its irresistible advance. Its complete ascendency, however, was not established until long after the time of Chaucer. During the Wars of the Roses, the language manifested a strong tendency to resolve itself into its dialectic forms. Northern terms and idioms again appeared, and it was reserved for a Kentish man and his printing-press to consummate the task which had been commenced by Robert of Brunne and continued by Wycliffe and Chaucer. The East Midland dialect, as we have pointed out, had assumed a simple analytic form, like our modern English. This was in great measure owing to its attrition with the Danish speech and the consequent falling away of its inflections. It had largely absorbed the French element, had been cultivated by Orm, a rare genius and our first orthoepical reformer, and in the hands of Robert of Brunne it assumed a character which differs slightly from our modern idioms. In the time of Chaucer it had become the literary language of London and of Oxford, and was current among persons of courtly rank and in the higher classes of society. It combined all the essential elements of a great language. The vigour of the antique Roman, the heroic enterprise of the Dane, the versatile genius of the Norman, were felicitously blended in the composition of the races by whose commingling the speech of Spenser and of Shakspere was gradually formed. The French element had been in great measure introduced before the commencement of Chaucer's literary career, and was probably familiar to the greatest number of those for whom he wrote. We have elsewhere endeavoured to defend him from the old and oft-repeated complaint of corrupting the purity of his native tongue by the introduction of French words.

The necessities of metre and of rhyme, which had now become an established feature of English verse; the fearful losses which the poetic, moral, and intellectual vocabulary of Anglo-Saxon had sustained during the long period of its depression; its scarcity of rhyming words, rendered recourse to the tongue of France indispensable to poetic success. A large proportion of the French words employed by Chaucer and Gower are those which have the rhyming syllables at the end of the lines. Chaucer, then, did not introduce into the English tongue French words which it already rejected, but he impressed the greater part of those previously in use with the sanction of his authority, and thus invested them with all the rights of native-born English vocables. He was not the creator of our vocabulary, but rather its umpire or arbiter, and by his happy faculty of selection and his appreciation of the necessities of the speech, he constructed out of existing materials a literary diction which, in all the essentials of poetic art, was, at that era, unsurpassed in any of the cultivated languages of Europe. The excellence of Chaucer's judgment, and his perfect comprehension of the needs of the language, are strikingly illustrated by the fact that, of the French words found in his writings, not much above one hundred have become obsolete,* while a much greater num-

---

* Of the French words introduced by Langlande, many took no root, such as *brocage, creaunt, fenestres, devoir, losengerie*. In sentiment and poetic spirit there is a much closer connection between

ber of Anglo-Saxon words contained in his works have fallen completely into disuse. In fact, the number of French words introduced by Chaucer is much fewer than is commonly supposed, and his rare discrimination is manifest in his selection of native as well as of foreign terms. English he employed from preference; French, from the metrical defects of the Saxon and the consequent necessity for recourse to French models of versification; and his deviations from the pure English idiom are of rare occurrence. The language of Gower does not differ essentially from that of his great contemporary. It is not so purely English in style, and it contains a larger proportion of French words. His real merit is that of a linguistic refiner, rather than a poet of genuine excellence; and his precise and accurate rhyme exercised a marked influence in moulding and determining the literary form of the language.

Piers the Plowman and Chaucer than exists between Chaucer and Gower, who have little in common except that they compose in the same language, and in a style different from their contemporaries and predecessors. The true distinction between Langlande and Chaucer is linguistic rather than poetic; the former seems to have blended imperfectly the conflicting elements in the vocabulary, while his illustrious successor has fused them so skilfully and harmoniously, that the foreign terms appear as native-born words. The one was a genuine poet; the other was not only a poet, but a word-artist of unsurpassed penetration and perception.

CHAPTER XII.

THE AGE OF CHAUCER AND GOWER (*continued*).

UNDER the guidance of Chaucer, the tongue of England advanced at once to that preëminence which it maintains among the languages of Europe. Its vocabulary, hitherto unregulated and fluctuating, was now reduced to order; one form of speech constituted the standard of literary composition; its metrical capabilities were tested and expanded; the age of English literature had fairly commenced.

We are now in a position to understand the true relation of English to its various patois or provincial dialects. The patois were those dialects of the language which received no perceptible infusion of French, but remained unaffected by foreign admixture. It must not be supposed, however, that they passed into mere provincial forms without leaving any distinct impression upon the standard speech. On the contrary, many of the characteristic peculiarities of the literary idiom are traceable to dialectic influence. Their impress is especially perceptible in our complex and discrepant system of orthography, whose anomalies are clearly due to the fusion of many dialects into one, and the preservation in the standard tongue of their orthographical diversities and discordances.

The writings of Chaucer and Gower were the first specimens of truly national as well as truly English literature. An harmonious and generally received language, a unity of national spirit, writings comprehensive in their scope and character, and discussing topics intelligible to the majority of educated persons, are the indispensable conditions of a truly national literature. These conditions were fulfilled during the latter half of the fourteenth century, and in great measure by the influence of Chaucer and Gower. It is from this period that we must date the commencement of that magnificent and incomparable literature which is the richest inheritance of the English-speaking race.

The poetic models upon whom Chaucer founded his style were principally those of France. They were everywhere, perhaps, still regarded as the classic poetry of modern times; and the younger poetry of Italy, which was derived from the same common source, had not, with all its excellence, either supplanted the ballads and romances of the trouvères and troubadours, or even attained a corresponding eminence. The earliest English, as well as the earliest Italian, poetry was principally imitated or translated from that of France. The greater part of the poetry written in the French language during the eleventh, twelfth, and thirteenth centuries, was written in England for English readers, and to a considerable extent by native poets. French poetry, during this period, does not appear to have been regarded as a foreign literature, and even at a subsequent era it must have been considered by every cultivated Englishman as properly belonging to his own land. For a hundred years before the time of Chaucer, perhaps even longer, the majority of English versifiers had been occupied in translating the French romances into English, now gradually, but steadily, becoming the common speech of the educated. These translations were executed with little accuracy, and were designed merely to render the meaning of the original intelligible to the English reader. During the latter half of the fourteenth century, at which time Chaucer began to write, the French had nearly disappeared as a general medium of communication; the English, on the contrary, had improved decidedly in precision, regularity, and in general adaptation to the purposes of literary composition.* Chaucer was probably more indebted to the Troubadour or Provençal poets than to any other foreign sources, for polished and appropriate models of poetic style. Under the guidance of this wonderful race of minstrels, poetry had attained an artistic elegance and perfection unsurpassed, if not unapproached, in ancient or modern ages, and from the lovely land of Provence the inspiration of the Muse had extended into many distant climes; the Troubadour poetry supplied the models upon which that of Germany, Italy, and that of their successors, the Trouvères of Northern France, were constructed. Their influence upon the literature of mediæval Europe was immense; they were the acknowledged standards of poetic excellence, and it was among them that the literature of modern times first appeared, radiant with hope and vigour, after the long and dreary period that had intervened since the fall of the Roman Empire.

The two periods in Provençal or Troubadour history extend from the second half of the eighth century to 1080, and from 1080 to 1350. Of these, the second is

---

* Craik's English Literature.

by far the more important, as it was during this era that the Provençal poetry flourished in its greatest excellence and popularity. The Anglo-Norman literature, introduced into England by the conquerours, had two points of contact with the Provençals; one of which was furnished by its general and indirect relations to France; the other, through the Kings of England, who had become Dukes of France, and who maintained habitual communication with several of the provinces of the South. The literature of the Provençals had thus two avenues open by which to penetrate into Great Britain. Henry II. and his sons distinguished themselves by their zeal for the encouragement of the Troubadours. His queen, Eleanor of Guienne, drew several of them after her, and, among others, one of the most famous, Bernard de Ventadour. Notwithstanding these propitious influences, the Provençals exerted but little effect upon the Anglo-Norman literature. The latter can show nothing which can be compared with the lyrical productions of the former. As to poetical romances, the Anglo-Normans composed several of them, they translated others, and they were acquainted with several more through the medium of French translations. By the side of this Anglo-Norman literature, which was properly that of the court and the conquerours, there arose another in the language of the country, and this was the literature of the people. The Provençal literature is more apparent in the latter than in the former.* It was upon the models furnished by these brilliant and gifted versifiers that Chaucer refined our native tongue, smoothed down its roughness, expanded its capabilities,

---

* Fauriel's "History of Provençal Literature."

developed its metrical powers, and polished its modes and styles of versification.

As we have already pointed out, alliteration was the essential characteristic of Anglo-Saxon verse, though rhyme was occasionally employed. Rhyme appears to be the form which poetry spontaneously assumes; it is, in fact, coeval with poetry itself.' Its existence was as well known to Virgil and Horace as to Dryden and Pope. It was resorted to in ancient Roman poetry, both in compositions of an elevated and dignified character, and in caricature, satire, and ribaldry. "It may be discovered in Homer, in Æschylus, in Horace, and Ovid. Its employment is commented upon by Cicero and Quintilian, and the Greek rhetoricians. It is found in Prudentius, in Leo Diaconus, and in nearly all the intervening Latin poets, before it appears in full blossom in the hymns of the middle ages. With the disregard of quantity, the obscuration of inflections, and the increasing instability of accent, among mixed and imperfectly educated races, rhyme became a customary and almost indispensable ornament of verse in the later Latin and Greek." But in the classic poetry of antiquity, the rhythmical principle exerted too great an influence to allow the rhyme, as a rhetorical element, to attain that influence which it gained by a natural process when verses began to be measured according to the modern principle of rhetorical accent. Rhythm showed its influence in ancient poetry, not only in the single verses, but in the composition of several verses of a different size and fall, into an organic whole—the strophe. To the inheritance of the strophe, and its development into the stanza, mediæval poems, and especially the canzas of the Troubadours, owe their greatest interest. To the relics of ancient literature, already mentioned, was added the rhyme, defined by strict rules and made obligatory, and this new principle contributed not a little to give variety and harmony to the highest development of mediæval poetry, the stanza.*

In Saxon poetry, alliteration constituted the chief metrical characteristic, but even there, rhyme was occasionally employed, and it is assuming too much to assert that English poetry is entirely indebted to Norman-French for its introduction, as it was known and practised to some extent before the Conquest.† Among the earlier examples of its use, may be mentioned the Anglo-Saxon rhyming poem, discovered by Conybeare, and written about the close of the tenth century; lines in rhyme in the Anglo-Saxon Chronicle, upon the death of William the Conquerour; and a rhyming canticle, composed before 1170. In the reign of Henry II., Layamon's "Chronicle of Brutus" appeared, which contained occasional specimens of rhyming verse.

From the end of Henry III.'s reign ‡ to the middle of the fourteenth century, soon after which time Chaucer began to write, the number of English rhymers had greatly increased. In addition to several with whose names we are acquainted—Robert of Gloucester, Robert of Brunne, Richard Rolle, the Hermit of Hamphole,

---

* *North British Review*, January, 1871.

† Otfrid of Weissenberg, who flourished about 870, was the earliest rhymer in any of the modern languages of Europe.

‡ The decline in English rhyme, from the time of Henry II. to the end of Henry III.'s reign, is accounted for by the supposition that during this period the poets, who wrote for the fashionable, composed in French, scholars in Latin, while the Saxon poetry, being intended for the ignorant classes, was of a very inferior character, and has fallen into oblivion.—*Tyrwhitt's Introduction to Chaucer.*

and Lawrence Minot—it is probable that many of the anonymous authors, or rather translators of the popular poems, called Romances, existed during this era. As their poems were intended for recitation, perhaps to be accompanied by music, they probably were more attentive to the metre than to the rhyme.

Such was the general condition of English poetry about the time that Chaucer entered upon his literary career. Rhyme was gradually becoming a feature of versification, and was perhaps as generally recognized as blank verse was, at the time that Shakspére commenced the writing of his dramas. Although its introduction was not due to Norman-French poetry, its general acceptance and popularity were greatly accelerated by its superior adaptation to the purposes of metrical composition in a language like the French, in which the stress or emphasis is placed near to the ultimate syllable, or upon it.

After a short and ineffectual struggle, as well as an attempt at compromise, between the ancient alliterative system and the new rhyming verse, the latter prevailed, and maintained the ascendency until the latter decades of the sixteenth century.

So far as rhyme was concerned, little remained to be done by Chaucer except to lend the sanction of his authority to the example of his predecessors, and by his influence rhyming verse was firmly established as an essential element in our poetry. The metrical part of our language was capable of improvement by refining the modes of versification already adopted, as well as by the introduction of new styles. In this regard, Chaucer rendered illustrious service. He was the introducer of the heroic metre, and our metrical forms, inspired with new life by his talismanic touch, rang out with sweet notes, as clear and unfading, after the flight of five centuries, as the images of the Canterbury pilgrims.

Having thus traced the rise and formation of the King's English, under the guidance of Chaucer, and, in a less degree, of Gower, let us see if we may not at least catch the echo of those melodious sounds whose dulcet symphonies preluded the future glories of the English tongue.

CHAPTER XIII.

THE PRONUNCIATION OF THE ENGLISH LANGUAGE IN THE AGE OF CHAUCER.

With regard to the pronunciation of Anglo-Saxon, little can be ascertained. It is probable that it resembled that of Latin, and its accentual system, which placed the stress of the voice upon the root, and not upon the inflected syllables, caused the first syllables to be more forcibly enunciated than the last. In this respect it presented a direct contrast to the French, which tended to place the stress of the voice toward the end of the word. By the influence of the Norman Conquest, a new accentual system was introduced, which, towards the close of the twelfth century, began to manifest itself in the written speech. The vocabulary of the French language is, to a great extent, composed of Latin words which have lost their inflectional endings, generally the atonic or unaccented syllables. For example, the French noun, *réception*, is derived from the accusative case of the Latin noun, *reception-em*, by rejecting the inflected or unaccented syllable. The accented syllable of the Latin thus became the final syllable of the French word, and also the one upon which the stress of the voice was laid. When such words were transferred from French to English, they brought with them their native accentuation; and as accent is much stronger in English than in French, the final syllable was doubtless much more distinctly pronounced in the former than in the latter language.

By the introduction of the accentual system of the French tongue, a disturbing element entered into our orthoëpy, and the contest between the Gothic and Romance tendencies in English is not yet harmoniously concluded. French accentuation even affected pure English words; and we find *wisliche'* for *wis'liche*, *begyn'ning'*, *endyng'*, *absence'*, *mercy'*, *prayer'*, *conquerour'*, etc. Many French words, when Anglicized, receive a variable accent, as *for'tune*, *fortune'*, *con'tre*, *contree'*, *stat'ue*, and *statue'*.*

In the days of Chaucer, the pronunciation of English, so far as it is now possible to reclaim it, seems to have been as follows:

A=ah, as in *father;* the Latin and Continental sound of *a*. The present sound of *a*, as in *wait, late*, was not established until the beginning of the eighteenth century. A short=ăh, the short sound of *ah*, not now used in received English, but common in the provinces, Continental short *a*. The present very different pronunciation, as *a* in *cat*, was not in vogue until the seventeenth century. Aa, the same as a long. Ai=*ah'ee*, a diphthong, consisting of *ah*, pronounced briefly, but with a stress, and gliding on to *ee* in one syllable; the German sound of ai, and the French aï. The modern sound of ai, as in wait, was not in use before the seventeenth century. Au=ah'oo, a diphthong consisting of ah, pro-

---

* This will be apparent to any one who will observe the varying pronunciation of such words as contem'plate, con'template, demon'strate, dem'onstrate, con'versant, convers'ant, etc. It was only in the last generation that Rogers remarked, "Bal'cony (pronounced before balco'ny) is bad enough, but con'template makes me sick." In the United States, this tendency to place the accent as far as possible from the end of the word is especially marked.

nounced briefly, but with a stress, and gliding on to oo in one syllable; not now in use; the German au, the French aou. The modern sound of au, as Paul, was not established until the seventeenth century. Aw= Au. Ay=Ai.

B was pronounced as at present.

C=k before a, o, u, or any consonant, and equal to s before e, i, y. It was never sounded sh, as in the present sound of vicious, which then formed three distinct syllables, vi-ci-ous. Ch was pronounced as ch, in such, cheese.

D was pronounced as at present.

E long, as e in there, ai in pair, a in dare; that is, as ai is now pronounced before r, or rather more broadly than before any other consonant, and without any tendency to run into ee, nearly French e. The sound of e in eel was not established until the beginning of the eighteenth century. E short, like e in met, pen, e final, like ë, or short e, lightly and obscurely sounded, as the final e in the German einë, "herrliche," "gute," gabë. This sound was always used in prose when final e was the mark of some final vowel in older forms of the language, when it marked oblique cases, feminine genders, plural inflections of verbs, etc. But in poetry it was regularly elided altogether before a following vowel, and before *he, his, him, hire,* equal to her, here equal to their, hem equal to them, and sometimes before *hath,* hadde, have, hem, here, equal to here. It was never sounded in hire equal to her, here equal to their, oure equal to our, youre equal to your, and was often omitted in hadde equal to had, were, time, more. It was seldom omitted when necessary for the rhyme and metre, and for force of expression in other positions, especially when it replaced an older vowel, or marked an oblique case, as in German. Its pronunciation fell into disuse during the fifteenth century. Ea had the same sound as long e, like ea in break, great, wear; it was seldom used except in ease and please. The modern sound of ea, as ee in eel, was not in vogue until the eighteenth century. Ee the same as long e, as e'e in e'er, it frequently occurs. The modern sound of ee was not in general use before the middle of the sixteenth century; ei equal to ai, with which it is often interchanged by scribes. The modern sound, as ee, dates from the eighteenth century. Eo equal to long e, seldom used but in people, often spelled *pepel*. The modern sound of eo, as ee, came into use during the sixteenth century. Es final, mark of the plural, was generally sounded as es or is. Eu equal to ui in Scotch puir, the long sound of French u, German ü in all words of French origin. This assumed the sound of our modern eu in the seventeenth century. In words not derived from French, eu equal to ai′oo, a diphthong consisting of ai, pronounced briefly, but with a stress, and gliding on to oo in one syllable, as in Italian Europa. Ew equal ui in Scotch puir, or else ai′oo precisely as eu. Ey, the same as ay, with which it is constantly interchanged by scribes. The modern sound, as ee, belongs to the eighteenth century.

F, as at present.

G, equal to g hard in all *non*-French words; equal to j before e, i, in words of French origin. Ge final, or before a, o, in French words equal to j; the e is sometimes omitted. Gh equal to kh, the Scotch and German sound of ch.

H, initial, as at present, but probably generally omitted in unaccented he, his, him, hire equal to her, hem equal to them, and often in *hath, hadde, have,* just as we still have, I've told 'em, and in some French words, as host, honour, etc., probably omitted as now. H final represents a very faint sound of the guttural kh, into which it dwindled before it became entirely extinct.

I long was not at all the modern sound of i; it was the lengthened sound of i in still, almost, but not quite, ee; compare still and steal in saying, *Still* so gently o'er me *steal*ing; I short equal to i in pin, pit; I consonant equal to j. Ie, the same as long e, with which it is often interchanged. The modern sound of e dates from the seventeenth century.

K, as at present.

L, as at present. Lh equal to simple l.

M, as at present.

N, as at present; not nasalized in French words as now. Ng had three sounds as at present; as in *sing,* singer, *linger, change.*

Oa equal to a in boar, o in more, with a broader sound than *oa* in moan, or *o* in stone. O short equal to ŏa, the Continental short *o,* but not so broad as modern *o* in got, which was not established till the seventeenth century. Oa probably not in Chaucer; it was introduced for long o in the sixteenth century. Oe occurs very rarely; same as long *e.* Oi equal to oo'ee, a diphthong consisting of the sound of oo pronounced briefly, but with a stress, gliding on to ee in one syllable. Oo equal to long o; often interchanged with it. The modern sound of *oo* in pool dates from the middle of the sixteenth century. Ou had three sounds which may be thus distinguished: ou equal to oo, where it is now pronounced as in *loud;* ou equal to ŭ, where it is now pronounced as in *double;* ou equal to oa'oo, where it is now sometimes pronounced *oh'oo*, as in *soul.* Ow equal to ou. Oi equal to oi.

P, as at present. Ph equal to f, as now.

Qu, as at present.

R, as in ring, herring, carry; always trilled; never now as in car, serf, third, cord. Re final, probably the same as *er*, except when ë was inflectional. Rh equal to r, as at present.

S was more frequently a sharp *s* when final; then *was, is,* all had *s* sharp. But between two vowels, and when the final *es* had the *e* omitted after long vowels or voiced consonants, it was probably z, a letter sometimes interchanged with *s*, but rarely used. S was never *sh* or zh, as at present; thus, vision had three syllables, vi-si-on. Sch equal to sh in shall. Sh as now.

T, as at present, but final *tion* was in two syllables, *si-ion*. Th had two sounds, as in *thine, then;* probably sounded as now.

U long occurred only in French words, and had the sound of French u, German ü. The modern sound of *u* in tune was not introduced until the seventeenth century.

V consonant equal to v. V vowel equal to u. V consonant, as at present.

W vowel was used in diphthongs as a substitute for u, and sometimes absolutely for oo, as wde equal to oodë; herberw equal to *herberoo*. W consonant, as at present.

Y vowel, long and short, had just the same sound as I long and short. Y consonant, probably as now.

Z equal to z, as now, and never zh.*

---

* Ellis's Early English Pronunciation; Morris's Chaucer.

CHAPTER XIV.

THE VOCABULARY OF THE ENGLISH LANGUAGE.

HAVING traced the historical development of the English tongue from its crude beginnings among the Germanic and Scandinavian colonists of Angle-land to the period of its full fruition under the culture of Chaucer, Gower, and Wycliffe, we must endeavour to ascertain, as accurately as possible, the elements by whose blending the language was gradually formed, the time, the manner, and the conditions of their introduction.

The vocabulary of the English language, while it has incorporated elements drawn from nearly all the known languages of the world, is principally composed of Teutonic or Germanic, Keltic, Latin, and Romance constituents. We shall consider them principally with reference to the period of their introduction, and in the following order: First, the Keltic; Second, the Latin, with its Romance descendant, the French; Third, the Saxon or Germanic; Fourth, the Danish or Scandinavian; Fifth, the Greek; Sixth, the words derived from miscellaneous sources.*

---

* In enumerating the elements of the vocabulary, I have thought it best to classify French as part of the *indirect* Latin element, although it necessitates a departure from the chronological order, Saxon, in point of time, coming before French.

The Keltic.

It is a prevalent misapprehension that the Kelts, the primitive inhabitants of Britain, were almost extirpated by the Saxon invaders, and that the language and the people faded away without leaving a perceptible impression upon the tongues and the nationalities by which they were supplanted. But this is at variance with the facts; many local names in England, and some in America, attest the influence of the Keltic races, and remind us forcibly of their long sway in those lands in which English is now the dominant speech, while the number of designations of the most common articles, occurring in every day's ordinary intercourse, strikingly recalls their memory and their presence.

Local names derived from Keltic: *Avon, Derwent, London, Ouse, Medlock; Aber*, prefixed to names of places on or near the water, *Aberdeen, Aberconway, Havre; Yar* or *Gar*, in *Yarborough, Yarmouth, Yarcombe;* the same word occurs in *Garonne*, Garumna river; *Penrose, Pendell, Torbay, Torquay, Arden, Ardennes; Nant*, in *Nantes, Bangor;* Isle of *Wight*, Isle of *Man*.

A number of Keltic terms were introduced into Anglo-Saxon, and have thus passed over into the English. Such are, brock (badger), breeches, clout, cradle, crock, crook, glen, kiln, mattock.

Keltic words still existing in English: ballast, boast, bod-(kin), bog, bother, bribe, cam (crooked, used by Shákspere), crag, dainty, dandriff, darn, daub, dirk, gyve, havoc, kibe, log, loop, maggot, mop, motley, mug, noggin, nod, pillow, scrag, spigot, squeal, squall.

Keltic words of recent introduction: bannock, bard,

brogue, clan, claymore (great sword), clog, log, Druid, gag, pibroch, plaid, pony, shamrock, slab, whisky.

A number of Keltic words were brought over to England in the Norman-French tongue, and consequently perpetuated in the English. The Northern French, which was a Neo-Latin dialect, contained several thousand Keltic words, many of which are retained in the standard French language. The widely extended predominance of the Keltic, its contact, and to some extent, its commingling with the Latin, produced by war, conquest, and colonization, caused it to enter into the Neo-Latin or Romance dialects, as a modifying element; and it may be laid down as a general rule, that whatever grammatical differences exist between the ancient Latin and the Neo-Latin tongues of Gaul, are traceable to its influence.* Many of the characteristic peculiarities of the French are clearly of Keltic origin. Again, as nearly all French words, not derived from Latin or Teutonic sources, have their roots in the Keltic, so nearly all English words, not derived from the Teutonic, the French, the classic languages, the Scandinavian tongues, nor from the miscellaneous sources hereafter to be indicated, are of Keltic origin.

Keltic words introduced by Norman-French: bag, barren, barter, barrator, barrel, basin, basket, bassinet, bonnet, bucket, boots, bran, brisket, button, chemise, clapper, dagger, gravel, gown, harness, marl, mitten, motley, osier, pot, possnet, rogue, ribbon, skain (skein), tike.

LATIN OF THE FIRST PERIOD, B. C. 55–A. D. 447.

The Latin words in the vocabulary of the English language were introduced at different epochs, and under

---

* Schneider, Geschicte der Englischen Sprache.

different linguistic, literary, and political conditions. The First Roman Period embraces the interval between the invasion of Britain by Julius Cæsar, B. C. 55, and the final withdrawal of the Roman legions, A. D. 447.

With regard to the Latin words introduced during this period, a diversity of opinion exists. The majority of the historians of the language, and of writers upon the Science of Language, incline to the belief, that, except a few military terms and local names—stratum, street, (Stratford), cester, castrum, Lancaster, Gloucester, coln, colonia, Lincoln, pont, pons, Pont-e-fract, (Pom-fret)— our tongue received no accessions from the Latin during the long period of Roman dominion. But with all possible deference to the judgments of the accomplished scholars who adopt this view, it seems unsupported by trustworthy historical testimony, and directly at variance with the evidence of the language itself.

The general diffusion of the Latin language was one of the most potent auxiliaries employed by the Roman power in the extension of its sway, and in assimilating the conquered provinces to the Roman character.* Community of language and of laws constituted a powerful instrument in welding together into a coherent and organized mass the various races and nationalities, over

---

* " Rarely, if ever, did the barbarian conqueror dare, when acting as a ruler, to speak his native language ; he endangered his royal caste unless he comported himself like a Roman on the throne ; the very sound of the Latin language implied supremacy and command. The Latin was the only recognized vehicle of official business in the Romano-barbarian states ; the sovereigns of Teutonic blood promulgated their laws, asserted their prerogatives, bestowed their bounties, or rebuked their people, in the language of the Cæsars. Capitulars, statutes, rescripts, charters, all public documents, are written in Latin."—*Palgrave's Anglo-Saxon Commonwealth.*

which the symbols of her empire were gradually extending. The Latin by degrees supplanted the native dialects throughout the provinces, and there is no reason that Britain should have formed an exception to the general rule. The historical testimonies are abundant to the effect that Britain was thoroughly Romanized, and received an abiding impress of Roman arts, culture, and language. After the reign of Claudius, the rigour of Roman tyranny seems to have yielded to a milder and more tolerant policy; and when the privileges of Roman citizenship were conferred upon all the Provincials by Caracallus, the Briton entered upon the possession of his rights without molestation. The long intervals of silence respecting the affairs of Britain, attest the tranquillity of the island, and the prosperity of its inhabitants, consequent upon the relaxation of Roman rule, and there are many unmistakable indications of friendly intercommunication between conquerors and conquered. The readiness with which the islanders acquired the language, as well as the arts, the culture, and the elegancies of the capital, is especially commented upon by Tacitus, and seems to have excited his wonder, if not to have aroused his suspicion. The Latin tongue, the great medium of literature, of diplomacy, and of intercourse, was acquired with eagerness, and the youth of Britain became ambitions of excelling in eloquence. In Gaul it had superseded the Keltic, and the forensic skill of the Gauls passed over the Channel into the neighbouring land. It was almost impossible that Britain should not have been imbued with a strong colouring of the Roman tongue; and we discover that a very considerable number of words, names of trees, flowers, herbs, designations of weights and measures, and of the ordinary appliances of daily life, were introduced into the Keltic tongue from Rome, transferred to the Anglo-Saxon invaders by the Romanized Briton, and are thus perpetuated in the vocabulary of the English language.* The following are the Latin terms introduced into the island during the First Roman Period.

Anglo-Saxon.	Latin.	English.
Ince,	Ulna,	Ell.
Mil,	Mille (passuum),	Mile.
Carta,	Charta,	Paper.
Pinn,	Penna,	Pen.
Line,	Linea,	Line.
Circol,	Circulus,	Circle.
Demum,	Damnum,	Damage.
Profian,	Probare,	Prove.
Wed,	Vadium,	Pledge.
Sign,	Signum,	Sign.
Cóc,	Coquus,	Cook.
Cycene,	Coquina,	Kitchen.
Disc,	Discus,	Dish.

---

* As a proof of the extent to which Britain had become Romanized, it may be said, that boxes of Roman quack medicines are still disinterred, and spurious coin is found in quantities that induce us to regard it as a device of the imperial treasury. There was no country which received a deeper impression from Roman civilization and Roman architecture than Britain. The stately towers, the theatres, the baths, which remained undestroyed for centuries, exciting the wonder of the chronicler and the traveller; the edifices which, even in the fourteenth century, were so numerous and so magnificent as almost to surpass any others on this side of the Alps; the numerous legends respecting the Trojan origin of the Britons, strikingly attest the abiding influence of the Roman occupation, the intercommunication and commingling of Kelt and Roman, and the consequent effect of the speech of the victors upon the speech of the vanquished. Upon these points I would advise the student to consult Pearson's "England in the Middle Ages," and Palgrave's "Anglo-Saxon Commonwealth."

Anglo-Saxon.	Latin.	English.
Taefl,	Tabula,	Table.
Setl,	Sedile,	Seat.
Synder,	Cineres,	Ashes.
Cyse,	Caseus,	Cheese.
Ele,	Oleum,	Oil.
Eced,	Acetum,	Vinegar.
Win,	Vinum,	Wine.
Ostre,	Ostreum,	Oyster.
Cancer,	Cancer,	Crab.
Candel,	Candela,	Candle.
Cyl,	Culeus,	Sack.
Cyst,	Cista,	Chest.
Socc,	Soccus,	Sock.
Ongul,	Angulus,	Hook.
Balistas,	Balista,	Balista.
Ceaster,	Castrum,	Camp.
Port,	Portus,	Port.
Straet,	Strata,	Street.
Weall,	Vallum,	Wall.
Mur,	Murus,	Wall.
Tempel,	Templum,	Temple.
Scólu,	Schola,	School.
Cite,	Civitas,	City.
Municep,	Municipium,	A borough.
Carcern,	Carcer,	A prison.
Camp,	Campus,	A field.
Aecer,	Ager,	A sown field.
Munt,	Mons,	Hill (mount).
Funt,	Fons,	Fountain.
Lac,	Lacus,	Lake.
Baron,	Vir, varo,	A man.
Wencle,	Ancilla,	Maid.
Wydewe,	Vidua,	Widow.
Sol,	Solea,	A sole or sandal.
Scol-maegistre,	Scholæ magister,	Schoolmaster.
Mynet,	Moneta,	Mint.
Púnd,	Pondus,	Pound.
Elu,	Ulna,	Ell.
Ince,	Uncia,	Ounce.
Pil,	Pilum,	Dart.

THE VOCABULARY OF THE ENGLISH LANGUAGE. 119

ANGLO-SAXON.	LATIN.	ENGLISH.
Craesta,	Crista,	A crest.
Geoc,	Iugum,	Yoke.
Calc,	Calc,	Lime.
Tem,	Temo,	Team.
Spád,	Spata,	Spade.
Fann,	Vannus,	Fan.
Forc,	Furca,	Fork.
Maeth,	Messis (meto),	A mowing.
Pic,	Pix,	Pitch.
Fraene,	Frænum,	Rein.
Aer, es,	Æs, æris,	Brass.
Tigol,	Tegula,	Tile.
Ancer,	Anchora,	Anchor.
Ort-geard,	Hortus,	Garden, orchard.
Rose,	Rosa,	Rose.
Lilie,	Lilium,	Lily.
Peru,	Pyrus,	Pear.
Fic,	Ficus,	Fig.
Casten-(bean),	Castanus,	Chestnut.
Persoc-(treow),	Persica,	Peach.
Mor-(beam),	Morus,	Mulberry.
Laur-(beam),	Laurus,	Laurel.
Pine-(treow),	Pinus,	Pine.
Bux,	Buxum,	Box-tree.
Lín,	Linum,	Flax.
Pipor,	Piper,	Pepper.
Pionie,	Pæonia,	Pæony.
Cucumer,	Cucumis,	Cucumber.
Cawe,	Caulis,	Cabbage.
Raedic,	Radix,	Radish.
Sin-fulle,	Cinquefolium,	Cinquefoil.
Mul,	Mulus,	Mule.
Stemn,	Stemma,	Stem.
Crisp,	Crispus,	Crisp.
False,	Falsus,	False.*

---

* Pearson's "England in the Early and Middle Ages." Appendix to Vol. I.

Latin of the Second Period.

The Anglo-Saxons were converted to Christianity about the close of the sixth century. Between that time and the Norman Conquest (1066), many Latin words were introduced, pertaining chiefly to ecclesiastical affairs and the ritual of the church. *Mynster*, a minster, *monasterium; portic*, a porch, *porticus; cluster*, a cloister, *claustrum; munuc*, a monk, *monachus; bisceop*, a bishop, *episcopus; arcebisceop*, archbishop, *archiepiscopus; sanct*, a saint, *sanctus; profost*, a provost, *propositus; pall*, a pall, *pallium; calic*, a chalice, *calix; psalter*, a psalter, *psalterium; maesse*, a mass, *missa; pistel*, an epistle, *epistola; praedician*, to preach, *prædicare*. Also the designation of some foreign plants and animals; *camell*, a camel, *camelus;* *elylp*, elephant, *elephas; peterselige*, parsley, *petroselinum; feferfuge*, feverfew, *febrifuga*.

Third Latin Period.—Mediæval Latinity.

The influence of the Mediæval Latinity has profoundly affected the vocabulary of the English language. Throughout the dark and middle ages Latin constituted the medium of jurisprudence, of theology, of the scholastic philosophy, and of science. The boundless variety of new conceptions, evoked by the new conditions of society in the process of transition from ancient to modern times, demanded adequate forms of expression. These could only be obtained by the creation of new words out of pre-existing Latin materials, a task which was gradually accomplished by the labours of the schoolmen, the ecclesiastics, the theologians, and the civilians. Hence arose that strange product known as Mediæval Latin, in which are embodied the far-reaching wisdom of Roger Bacon, the manly sentiments of Grostête, and which has tended essentially to enrich the vocabulary of the English tongue.*

Our Mediæval Latin words were principally introduced between the Conquest, 1066, and the Revival of Learning. Their number and character have not, thus far, been accurately determined.

Many Latin words were introduced by the chroniclers during the twelfth and thirteenth centuries. A large Latin element was indirectly introduced through the Norman-French, which was a Neo-Latin or Romance dialect.

FOURTH LATIN PERIOD.—FROM THE REVIVAL OF LITERATURE TO THE PRESENT TIME.

This includes the Latin words which originated in the writings of scholars, reformers, and of learned men in general. The words introduced during this period may be distinguished from those of the preceding: First. They

---

* The rise of theology, scholastic philosophy, and jurisprudence, demanded an immense number of new words for the adequate expression of the new ideas which they had called into existence. The Latin tongue was remarkably defective in abstract nouns; these were supplied principally by Tertullian and the Latin fathers; Jerome contributed powerfully to the formation of ecclesiastical Latin by his translation of the Scriptures into that language (Vulgate); the schoolmen introduced many philosophical terms; the civilians, many legal words and phrases. Latin was the general medium of learning and of science for a long period even after the Revival of Learning. It was within a comparatively recent era that the vernacular tongues of Europe were advanced to that preëminence which they occupy at present.

retain more accurately the form, and, in many cases, the inflections of the original language. Not having passed through the French, they are free from that compression and attenuation of form which is produced by the action of phonetic decay. Second. They relate to objects and ideas for which the increase in the range of science and of learning required expression. The Latin element introduced through the French, and that which is derived directly from the original, may be illustrated by comparing the following words.

Ancestor and *antecessor*, *sampler* and *exemplar*, *benison* and *benediction*, *conceit* and *conception*, *constraint* and *construction*, *defeat* and *defect*, *forge* and *fabric*, *integer* and *entire*, *invidious* and *envious*, *extraneous* and *strange*, *fact* and *feat*, *malison* and *malediction*, *mayor* and *major*, *nourishment* and *nutriment*, *poor* and *pauper*, *orison* and *oration*, *proctor* and *procurator*, *purveyance* and *providence*, *ray* and *radius*, *respite* and *respect*, *retreat* and *retract*, *sir* and *senior*, *surface* and *superficies*, *sure* and *secure*, *treason* and *tradition*.

From the Latin we obtain a large proportion of our moral and intellectual vocabulary, our terms for the expression of abstract relations and conceptions. The Latin words may generally be distinguished from those of native growth by the class of ideas which they denote, by their greater length (the Saxon words being on an average less than half as long as the Latin), and by their peculiar prefixes and suffixes, a list of which is inserted. Latin prefixes: *a, ab, abs,* from, as *a*vert, *ab*jure; *ad, a, ac, af, ag, al, an, ap, ar, as, at,* to, as *ad*duce, *ac*cede, *af*fix; *ante,* before, as *ante*cedent; *circum,* about, as *circum*jacent; *con, co, cog, col, com, cor,* together, with, as *con*form, *col*loquy, *co*eval; *contra,* against, as *contra*dict; *de*, down, from, as *de*scend, *de*fame; *dis*, asunder, as *dis*sever, *dis*rupt; *e*, *ex*, out of, *ex*pel, *e*ject; *extra*, beyond, as *extra*ordinary; *in*, *ig*, *il*, *im*, *ir* (when prefixed to a verb), in, as *in*duce; (when prefixed to an adjective), not, as *in*vidious; *inter*, between, as *inter*vene; *intro*, within, as *intro*duce; *ob*, *oc*, *of*, *op*, for, in the way of, as *op*pose, *of*fend; *per*, through, as *per*meate; *post*, after, as *post*script; *pre*, before, as *pre*cede; *preter*, beyond, as *preter*natural; *pro*, for, forward, *pro*ject, *pro*vide; *'re*, back, again, *re*mit, *re*turn; *retro*, backwards, as *retro*grade; *se*, aside, as *se*cede; *sine*, without, as *sine*cure; *sub*, *suc*, *suf*, *sug*, *sup*, *sus*, under, after, as *suc*ceed, *sub*altern, *suf*fice, *sug*gest, *sup*port, *sus*pect; *super*, above, as *super*sede; *trans*, beyond, as *trans*cend; *ultra*, beyond, as *ultra*montane. The following terminations are derived from the Latin or French: *able, ible, cle, ile, ial, al, ian, an, ant, ent, fy, lar, ity, or, ose, ous, sion, tion, tive, tude, ture.*

But the Latin has not merely furnished our intellectual and philosophical terms; it has thoroughly penetrated the structure of our tongue, and has assimilated itself to its genius and character, so that if the skeleton is Gothic, the texture is Romance and Latin. It has contributed essentially to the affluence of our speech in a great diversity of ways; to the dialect of busy, active life, of daily intercourse, to the vocabulary of the merchant, of the banker, and the mechanic, as well as to the stately and elaborate diction of the historian or the philosopher. Observe the vocabulary of the man of business, and see how large a proportion of it is drawn from the Latin: *account, balance, bank, banker, bankrupt, bill, cancel, calculate, capital, claim, clerk, count, compute, credit, currency, debt, debit, debtor, deficit, discount, due, entry, finance, fiscal, ink, invoice, interest, insure, insurance, liquidate, money, negotiate, note, pay, par, per cent., policy, premium, profit, security, sum, specie.*

The pre-eminently monosyllabic character of English is commonly attributed to the existence of the same feature in Anglo-Saxon, together with its method of inflection by letter change, and not by the addition of a formative element, *d* or *ed*. A more diligent examination, however, will convince us that our monosyllables are, to a considerable extent, due to the Latin, and that they are produced by the agency of sound decay, the consequent compression of syllables, rejection of medial consonants, and dropping of inflections. The following list of monosyllabic words derived from Latin, or from Latin through the French, some of which are designations of familiar objects and ordinary appliances, shows how largely the Latin has contributed to the *practical* vocabulary of our language, as well as to its intellectual wealth: *act, air, aunt, apt, art, arm, age, aim, bank, balm, bench, beat, box* (tree), *bill, bull, bowl, brief, cant, care, cure, cat, cave, clause, cell, cent, chest, crest, crisp, clock, chief, camp, carp, chart, chaste, cheese, cook, chance, car, course, clear, clerk, claim, count, cede, cease, chain, corpse, crown, close, cube, code, crate, case, crude, disk, dish, desk, deck, duct, duke, debt, doubt, due, date, dame, dire, edge, err, face, fact, feat, fig, feign, fame, fan, fate, fount, front, fail, fraud, form, fort, fruit, frail, fume, flame, fuse, fork, firm, few, grade, grain, grave, grand, gem, globe, grace, hour, ink, inch, isle, ire, join, joke, joy, joint, just, judge, lake, lamp, lance, land, large, lapse, line, lure, light, league, mass* (missa), *mass* (massa), *mere, merse, merge, mint, mule, monk, mile, muse, mob, move, new, neck, noun, oil, ounce, pay, pass, pace, pan, paint, pain, point, punch, par, peer, pear, peach, pen, pitch, plume, place, please, poor, plaint, peace, price, preach, prey, pray, post, parch, part, parse, pine* (tree), *porch, plain, plane, pest, press, print, prime, proof, prove, port, plank, plant, pall, pope, prone, prose, prude, pound, pure, pole, queer, quaint, quart, quest, rage, round, rein, rude, rare, raw, ruin, rose* (noun, not the preterite tense of rise), *rule, sack, seal, sign, sense, seat, siege, site, spend, state, stain, sting, stray, strict, string, sound, scarce, screen, search, sconce, scorch, sire, spy, sir, sure, sock, suave, soil, safe, surge, serve, serf, sole, stem, strange, scourge, style, sage, scale, scan, spade, sum, spice, scribe, spoil, square, star, team, tend, tempt, test, tin, thin, tile, toast, tract, trait, tribe, trite, use, urn, vast, vale, vile, vein, vain, vent, verge, verse, vest, vine, vice, wade, waste, wine, yoke.*

The French Element in English.

A great number of French words were introduced by the Conquest. To the Norman-French we are indebted for many of the terms relating to feudalism, to war, the church, the law, and the chase.

First. Aid, arms, armour, assault, banner, baron, buckler, captain, chivalry, challenge, fealty, fief, gallant, homage, lance, mail, march, soldier, tallage, truncheon, tournament, vassal.

Second. Altar, bible, ceremony, devotion, friar, homily, idolatry, interdict, penance, prayer, relic, religion, sermon, scandal, sacrifice, tonsure.

Third. Assize, attorney, case, chancellor, court, dower, damages, estate, fee, felony, fine, judge, jury, mulct, parliament, plaintiff, plea, plead, statute, sue, tax, ward.

Fourth. Bay, brace, chase, couple, copse, course, covert, falcon, forest, leash, leveret, mews, quarry, reynard, rabbit, tiercet, venison.

From the Norman-French period descended a great number of terms expressive of malignant passion and hatred. The bitterness and virulence aroused by foreign sway, the reciprocal hatred and distrust generated by the Conquest, are strikingly reflected in the speech of this era. Rascal, villain, ribald, ribaldry, descend to us from those days of mutual animosity and disparagement. "Almost all the sinister and ill-favoured words in the English language at the time of Shakspere owe their origin to this unhappy period."

The predominance of the French as the social language of Europe, as the language of fashion, of diplomacy, and etiquette, has from time to time caused the adoption of many French words, some of which have been completely naturalized, while others reveal their origin.

From the French our tongue has acquired much of its elegance and precision, many of its characteristic graces, and its faculty of indicating things naturally offensive or repugnant, whose direct mention would not comport with perfect delicacy, either of manner or expression. The Anglo-Saxon, notwithstanding its vigour and plasticity, lacked polish and refinement; its terms were direct, energetic, but often coarse and inelegant. This defect, certainly a serious one, the Latin and its French descendant have to a great degree remedied, and our accessions in this respect are among the most valuable contributions to the wealth of our language.

French words:—Aide-de-camp, accoucheur, accouchement, attaché, au fait, belle, bivouac, belles-lettres, billet-doux, badinage, blasé, bon mot, bouquet, brochure, bonhomie, blonde, brusque, busk, coif, coup, début, débris, déjeuner, dépôt, éclat, élite, ensemble, ennui, etiquette, entremêts, façade, foible, fricassée, goût, interne, omelet, naïve, naïveté, penchant, nonchalance, outré, passé, persiflage, personnel, précis, prestige, programme, protégé, rapport, redaction, renaissance, recherché, séance, soirée, trousseau.*

The vocabulary of French contains a number of words, Teutonic in origin, which were introduced by the Franks, a German tribe, and afterwards Romanized more or less to adapt them to the pronunciation of the Roman inhabitants of Gaul. From France they passed over to England, and have thus been perpetuated in the vocabulary of our tongue. Such words are *ambassador, attack, attire, balcony, belfry, bivouac, chamberlain, choice, defile, enamel, eschew, guide, guile, guise, haunt, herald, massacre, pocket, quiver, reward, ring, rob, seize, slate, towel, wage, ward.*

---

* Morris's " English Accidence."

CHAPTER XV.

THE VOCABULARY OF THE ENGLISH LANGUAGE (*continued*).

THE ANGLO-SAXON OR TEUTONIC ELEMENT IN ENGLISH.

THE Anglo-Saxon constitutes the groundwork, the material substratum, of the English tongue. Nearly all the distinctive characteristics of English grammar are derived from this source. The following are Saxon: First. The definite article, *the*, and the indefinite, *an, a*; all pronouns, personal, relative, demonstrative, etc., and the numerals. Second. All auxiliary and defective verbs. Third. Nearly all the prepositions, and the conjunctions. Fourth. Nouns forming their plurals by change of vowel, as *man, men*, etc. Fifth. Verbs forming their past tense by change of vowel (irregular verbs, *sing, sang, sung*). Sixth. Adjectives forming their degrees of comparison irregularly, *good, bad*; in short, all those peculiarities of our grammar generally designated irregular, which is merely an arbitrary expression to indicate ancient Saxon forms and usages, and to distinguish them from the later or regular formations.

Second. 1. Grammatical inflections; plural suffixes *s* and *en*. 2. Verbal inflections of past and present tenses of active and passive participles. 3. Suffixes denoting degrees of comparison.

Third. 1. Numerous suffixes of nouns, as *hood, ship, down, th, ness, ing, ling, king, ock*. 2. Of adjectives, as *ful, less, ly, en, ish, some, ward, y*. 3. Of verbs, as *en*. 4. Many prefixes, as *a,* al, be,* for, ful, on, over, out, under*. 5. The names of the three elements, *earth, fire, water* (air is Latin *aer*), and of their changes; the names of the heavenly bodies, *sun, moon*, etc., except star (Latin *sterula*); of many of the divisions of time, as *morning, evening, twilight, noon, night, day, sunrise, sunset*: some of these are probably of Latin origin, as *hour, hora*. From the Saxon we have acquired the names of many of the most striking natural phenomena, *heat, cold, light, frost, snow, hail, rain;* also the names of the most prominent and attractive objects in external nature, as *sea, land, hill, dale, wood, stream*. The Anglo-Saxon has also furnished us with the designations of most of the seasons, *summer, winter, spring, fall*, (*autumn* is from the Latin *auctumnus*), with the names of the organs of the body, the modes of bodily action and posture, the most familiar animals, many of the words employed in the ordinary intercourse of life, many of the terms pertaining to traffic, commerce, to the market, the work-shop, the farm. Also, the words acquired in infancy, the terms spontaneously evoked by the child in its earliest efforts to give expression to its dawning thoughts, the constituent parts of saws, maxims, and proverbs, are chiefly Anglo-Saxon. The names of the dearest relations, *father, mother,† sister, brother, husband, wife;* of the objects suggestive of the tenderest memories, the holiest affections, *home, hearth, fireside, child, kindred, friends*, are inherited from the Saxon. The names of the simpler emotions of the mind, terms

---

* *a* and *be* are sometimes Norse.

† *Grand father, grand mother*, are half Saxon, half Romance; *aunt, uncle*, entirely Romance.

of pleasantry, satire, indignation, invective, and anger, are principally of native growth. The designations of special modes of performing an action of specific processes, are mainly Saxon, while the generic or abstract terms are to great extent Latin. Thus, *move*, the general term, is Latin, but the specific and varied methods of performing the action are indicated by words of Saxon origin: *run, jump, skip, walk*, etc.*

The Anglo-Saxon was moulded and prepared for literary application by scholars who wrote and spoke Latin, and who regarded it as the standard of literary excellence; its literature is in great measure translated or imitated from the Latin. It cannot be questioned that Latin exercised a powerful influence in determining the character of Saxon, essentially modifying both its vocabulary and syntax, and assimilating it more and more closely, in spirit and in structure, to the imperial tongue. A large proportion of the Anglo-Saxon vocabulary finds its cognate words in the Latin dictionary, and there can exist no reasonable doubt that it was decidedly Romanized in character. Again, the Teutonic languages, by whose gradual commingling on the soil of Britain the Anglo-Saxon was formed, were indebted to the Latin, as were also the Keltic tongues. Roman conquest and colonization had made their impression upon the Teutonic dialects long before the Saxon invasions of Britain. In addition to its direct influence, the extent of which is not properly appreciated, the Latin has perceptibly affected nearly every language and dialect that has contributed to the formation of our varied and copious speech; it has imparted

---

* *Edinburgh Review*, 1839, 1859.

a tinge of its own colouring to nearly all the manifold tributaries, by whose commingling English has acquired its marvellous affluence, catholicity, and comprehensiveness. The Roman image is reflected in them all.

The Danish Element in the English Language.

The Danish invasions and occupations of England extend from A. D. 787 to A. D. 1042, at which time the Saxon government was restored. It was principally the Anglo-Saxon dialects, and not so much the literary speech or language of Wessex, that were affected by Danish influence. It does not appear that the Danes made any effort to extend or to perpetuate their tongue in England. The Saxons and the Scandinavian races were closely related in language as well as by blood; there was a Scandinavian element among the Saxon colonists of Britain, and it is highly probable that the speech of the two nations was mutually intelligible. The Saxon understood the Dane; the Dane, the Saxon. This opinion finds some confirmation in the well-known story of King Alfred, who entered the Danish camp in the guise of a minstrel, and sang his songs and recited his poems in the Anglo-Saxon tongue. This at least indicates that the two languages possessed marked resemblances. It was in the north of England that the Danish tongue made the deepest impression. Northumbria longest withstood the advance of the victorious Normans. The northern counties were not included in the great survey made by the Conquerour in 1085, and in these regions the traces of Danish influence are most strongly marked and enduring. Many Danish words are preserved in the Northumbrian speech, and many of their characteristic peculiarities of grammatical structure (in which they differ essentially from the standard English) are derived from the Scandinavian tongues. The Danish conquests and occupations seem to have affected the structure of the Anglo-Saxon more than the vocabulary. In the north and east of England the Saxon inflections were seriously modified by Danish influence; their decay was accelerated, so that in the thirteenth and fourteenth centuries nearly all the older inflections of nouns, verbs, and adjectives had disappeared, while in the south of England the old forms survived until a much later period, and many of them are still in existence. There are numerous traces of Scandinavian terms in the local nomenclature of England, in the Old English literature of the north of the island, as well as in the provincial dialects or patois of Northumbria.*

---

* Scandinavian words in the Northumbrian dialects:
Barkle, to stick to, to adhere, to cover over.
Brangle, to quarrel.
Bunt, to take home, pack up, make into a bundle.
Clatch, a brood of chickens.
Creel, a frame to wind yarn upon, English, reel.
Clem, to starve; "I'm almost clemmed," i. e., starved.
Crib, a rack.
Faddle, nonsense, trifling.
Flit, to move from place to place.
Gain, gainer, a cross cut.
Gawby, a clownish simpleton.
Kick, fashion, mode; "a new kick," i. e., fashion; Dan. s-kik.
Lam, to beat soundly, to chastise.
Mood, satiated.
Rostle, to ripen.
Scar, a steep, bare rock (Walter Scott, Lochinvar).
Slunt, to be idle.
Whack, a heavy blow.
Whip off, to go off quickly.
Yark, to strike hard.—*Schneider.*

THE VOCABULARY OF THE ENGLISH LANGUAGE. 133

Local names derived from Danish: the termination *by*=town, *Whitby, Grimsby, Rugby;* *by*-law, a town law. The ending *son*, in names of persons, is also Danish, as *Hobson, Johnson, Nelson;* the endings *gill* and *kirk*, as *Ormesgill, Ormeskirk*.

Words derived from Danish or Scandinavian:*

---

* Scandinavian peculiarities in the grammar of the Northumbrian dialects.—According to the census of 1861, the population of England was 18,954,444, of which Northumbria contained 5,580,834. It embraces more than one-fourth of the territory and the population of England, over which the influence of the Scandinavian settlers is still distinctly traceable. The Northumbrian dialects, though differing as to the number of words, have a grammatical system which is common to them all, though it departs in some respects from the grammar of written English. Perhaps their most remarkable characteristic is the definite article, or more properly the demonstrative pronoun *t*, which is an abbreviation of the old Norse neuter demonstrative *hit*. This is not an elision of the *he* from the article *the* (which is of old Frisic origin), as may be seen from the fact that all the Bonapartist versions* of Solomon's Song, second chapter, first verse, uniformly agree throughout England, where they abbreviate at all, by making *the* into *th'* by eliding the final *e*. We quote from the Westmoreland version (from the centre of Northumbria), which is well executed and idiomatic. We select as a fair specimen the second chapter, first verse, of Solomon's Song, which in the authorized version reads as follows: "I am the rose of Sharon, and the lily of the valleys." In the Westmoreland version it reads thus: "I's t' roaz o' Sharon, and t' lilly o' t' valleys." The districts in which the abbreviated article prevails are the counties of Central and South Durham, all Yorkshire, and nearly all Lancashire. The next characteristic is not so widely extended, being confined to about one-third of Northumbria. This is the substitution of *at* for the relative *that*. In the authorized version, Solomon's Song, second chapter, fourteenth verse, we read: "That art in the clefts of the rocks;" in the Westmoreland it is: "At's i' t

---

* Prince Lucien Bonaparte paid much attention to the study of the Northern English dialects, into which he caused the second chapter of Solomon's Song to be translated.

Abroad, aslant, athwart, bang, bask, bellow, bole (of a plant), *blunt, booty, bound* (for a journey), *brag, brink, bull, busk, cake, call, cast, clip, clumsy, cross, crook, cripple, cuff, curl, cut, dairy, dash, daze, dazzle, die, droop, dub, dull, fellow, fleer* (to deceive, Shakspere, Julius Cæsar), *flit, fond, fool, fro, froth, gable, gait, grovel, glow, hale* (to drag, Acts of the Apostles, eighth chapter, third verse), *hit, hut, hustings, irk, keg, kid, kindle, leap* (year), *low, loft, lurk, niggard, mump, mumble, muck, odd, puck* (goblin), *ransack, root, scald* (poet), *scare, scold, skull, scull, scant, skill, scrub, skulk, sky, sly, screw, sleeve, sledge, sled, sleek, screech, shriek, sleight, sprout, stagger, stag, stack, stifle, tarn* (a lake), *trust, thrive, thrum, unruly, ugly, uproar, window, windlass.**

---

grikes o' t' crags." The aphæresis does not properly belong before the *at*, as it is a pure Scandinavian word. In the use of the verb *to be*, the Northumbrian follows the Scandinavian. In the third person plural, present tense, they use the singular instead of the plural form, e. g., Horses *is* dearer than cows *is*. They inflect, I is, thou is, et cet., adhering to the Scandinavian rule. Another peculiarity is the use of *i* for in; this is pure Scandinavian, being still used in Icelandic, Danish, and Swedish. From these few citations, we may see the extent to which the Danish has penetrated the speech of Northumbria, as illustrated by five of the most common words in English, the representatives of *the, that, in, art*, and *am*. Their nouns have but one case, having dispensed with the possessive inflection; for instance, they say, my brother hat, instead of my brother's hat. Their syntactical structure is characterized by extreme brevity and simplicity, sometimes condensing into one word an idea which requires for its proper expression in English two or three. Thus, in Solomon's Song, "I am the," is expressed I'st. The adjectives are distinguished by double forms, and by the Scandinavian superlative form *st* instead of *est.—From "Transactions of the London Philological Society."*

* The third person plural of the verb to be, *are*, is Danish.

To the Greek language, the English is indebted for most of the nomenclature of the physical sciences, a great proportion of the vocabulary of theology, philosophy, and of the terms employed in all arts and sciences, as well as a number of familiar terms. The Greek has also indirectly affected the English through the medium of the northern tongues, whose character it sensibly modified in the earliest ages. By its wonderful plasticity and faculty of combination, the Greek supplies appropriate designations for many of the inventions, discoveries, and improvements in art and science: *e. g., barometer, thermometer, stereoscope, photograph, telescope*, etc.

Many terms pertaining to the vocabulary of philosophy, science, metaphysics, logic, have lost their purely technical import, and have passed into the language of literature and the speech of every-day life: *corollary, element, demonstrative, antipodal, atom, genus, inference, mean between extremes, diametrically opposite, positive, negative, inverse ratio, phenomenon, idea, qualitative, quantitative, species, zenith*, and many others which occur in the ordinary conversation of all-intelligent persons.

Words Derived from Miscellaneous Sources.

In addition to the constituents of the vocabulary already mentioned, our language has been enriched by the naturalization of numerous words from a variety of sources, many of which owe their introduction to the extension of commerce and the predominance of England as a commercial nation, as well as to the spirit of maritime enterprise which pre-eminently characterizes the English race.

Hebrew: Abbot, amen, cabal, cherub, jubilee, pharisaical, Sabbath, seraph, Shibboleth.

Arabic: Admiral, alchemy, alkali, alcohol, alcove, alembic, almanac, amulet, arsenal, artichoke, assassin, atlas, azure, bazaar, caliph, chemistry, cotton, cipher, dragoman, elixir, felucca, gazelle, giraffe, popinjay, shrub, sofa, syrup, sherbet, talisman, tariff, tamarind, zenith, zero. Arabian culture and science exercised a powerful influence upon the literature of the Middle Ages. Many of the words named in the text have come into English through one of the Romance dialects: admiral, artichoke, assassin, popinjay.

Persian: Caravan, chess, dervish, emerald, indigo, lac, lilac, orange, pasha, sash, shawl, turban, tafferty.

Hindu: Calico, chintz, dimity, jungle, boot, muslin, nabob, pagoda, palanquin, paunch, pundit, rajah, rice, rupee, rum, sugar, toddy.

Malay: Bantam, gamboge, orang outang, rattan, sago, verandah, tatoo and taboo (Polynesian), gingham (Java).

Chinese: Caddy, nankeen, satin, tea, mandarin.

Turkish: Caftan, chouse, divan, janissary, odalisk, saloop, scimitar.

American: Canoe, cocoa, hammock, maize, potato, squaw, tobacco, tomahawk, wigwam, yam.

Italian: Balustrade, bandit, brave, bust, canto, carnival, charlatan, domino, ditto, dilettante, folio, gazette, grotto, harlequin, motto, portico, stanza, stiletto, stucco, studio, tenor, umbrella, vista, volcano.

Spanish: Alligator, armada, cargo, cigar, desperado, don, embargo, flotilla, gala, mosquito, punctilio, tornado.

Portuguese: Caste, commodore, fetishism, palaver, porcelain.

Dutch: Block, boom, cruise, loiter, ogle, ravel, ruffle, scamper, schooner, sloop, stiver, yacht.

German: Landgrave, landgravine, loafer, waltz, cobalt, nickel, quartz, feldspar, zinc.*

The vocabulary of the English language contains about one hundred and four thousand words. This does not include many provincial forms and local usages which are currently employed. The English is formed by the gradual blending of a greater diversity of languages and dialects than has ever entered into the formation of any other speech. Its main constituents are the Romance and the Teutonic, but it has appropriated and assimilated materials from nearly all the languages of the globe. This, while it is the cause of its comprehensiveness, versatility, and far-reaching adaptation, affords also the satisfactory explication of its complexity, its anomalous orthoëpy, its discrepant orthography, its seeming transgressions of grammatical prescription. They constitute part of the exuberant wealth of our tongue; they have resulted from the peculiar historical conditions under which it was developed and matured. The kindred languages of Europe were founded either upon the Lingua Rustica or popular Latin as their basis, or upon a Teutonic or Scandinavian groundwork. But it is the especial glory of the English tongue to have blended the graces and the energy of the two most powerful languages of the Aryan family. It is in English, and in English only, that all the phonetic elements, the diverse and varied forms of the Aryan family have converged. After many centuries of separation, many strange wanderings in foreign lands, upon the soil of Angleland the long severed linguistic branches are peacefully reunited, enriched with the wisdom and the

---

* Morris's "English Accidence."

experience acquired by many painful vicissitudes, many diverse fortunes, since they parted at the base of their mountain homes and started out upon their marvellous career.

The greatest number of words in the vocabulary of the English language is derived from Romance and classical sources. This may at first sight appear contradictory and inconsistent, as the majority of persons, both in speaking and in writing, employ a greater number of Saxon than of Romance words; but it is the *character* of the objects denoted by these words, the necessity for their constant recurrence, and not their actual predominance, that give them a numerical superiority. Again: the conjunctions, the indispensable parts of a sentence, "its bolts and pins," are nearly all Saxon, so that it is almost impossible to compose the simplest sentence without employing the Saxon element.

But the greater proportion of the grace and refinement of our tongue, and consequently much of its superior adaptation to all the loftier purposes of literature, are attributable to its Latin and Romance constituents. If the Romance element were eliminated from our vocabulary, we should have a speech vigourous and energetic, but devoid of that delicacy of expression and rhythmical charm which so adorn the commonest utterances as well as the grandest climaxes of the orator, or the intricate details of the historian.

By its blending of two languages, English is enriched with a great variety of synonyms; we may, in fact, be said to have two languages in one; and this bilingual system has formed a distinctive feature of our tongue in all stages of its history, from the time that it was moulded into harmonious form by the delicate touch of

Chaucer's master hand. It is turned to good account by the translators of the Holy Scriptures, and much of the melodious rhythm that characterizes the Book of Common Prayer of the Anglican Church must be attributed to the judicious employment of Saxon and Romance synonyms.

CHAPTER XVI.

THE ENGLISH LANGUAGE FROM CHAUCER TO CAXTON.—
A. D. 1400-1474.

In the preceding chapters we indicated the manifold sources from which the constituents of our rich and varied vocabulary are derived. We must now retrace our steps, and resume our history at the period at which we for a time left it, the age of Chaucer, Gower, and Wycliffe. The era which was adorned by the genius of these illustrious names did not realize the bright promises to which it had pointed so auspiciously. When the political and religious distractions of the fourteenth century had subsided, the intellectual vigour and energy that characterized the age were succeeded by a long period of inactivity and depression. The original and creative power of the English mind seems to have disappeared, and much of the literature of this century consists of mere translations or imitations of older models.

The names of seventy poets have descended to us from this dreary period, of whom the most deserving of commemoration are Ocleve, James I. of Scotland, and Lydgate. All of these acknowledge Chaucer as their master and model in the poetic art.

The number of prose writers is very limited, and the development of a pure English prose style was reserved until after the introduction of printing should begin to exercise a decided influence upon the language. The prose writers of this period are principally theological. Bishop Pecoke, whose "Repressor" appeared in 1450, was the purest of these. His grammar is essentially the same as that of Wycliffe, with some tendency to greater simplification of structure, and a perceptible advance in style and construction. But in the main, the language seems to have retrograded, rather than to have advanced, between the death of Chaucer and the establishment of printing. The fierce and sanguinary Wars of the Roses, which extended over more than a quarter of the century —1455–1486—the convulsions and dissensions which disorganized the constitution of society, exerted for a time a most baneful influence upon the character of the tongue. Sympathizing with the vicissitudes of those who spoke it, and deprived of the conservative power of literary culture, it began to lose the coherence and the uniformity it had acquired under the skillful guidance of Chaucer, and manifested a marked tendency to disintegration, or resolution into its dialectic forms. But, notwithstanding the disastrous results that were temporarily produced by the protracted Wars of the Roses, their ultimate effects upon the fortunes and the constitution of the language were in many regards salutary and beneficial. The marching to and fro, throughout all portions of the kingdom, of vast bodies of men, the commingling of classes and dialects hitherto separate and isolated, the general intercommunication between sections of the island hitherto almost as unknown to their respective inhabitants as foreign lands, all tended in the end to impress upon the language, as well as upon the nation, a uniformity which strikingly contrasted with the diversity and confusion that had previously prevailed. In addition to this, the partial extirpation of the Norman nobility,* the elevation of the Saxon burghers in their stead, tended powerfully to efface the ancient distinction between the Norman lord and the Saxon vassal, which had its origin at the Conquest, to obliterate social distinctions, and thus efficaciously to promote uniformity of national character, as well as uniformity of speech. Hence, we discover that during this era, nearly the last vestiges of our inflexional system disappeared; local peculiarities, sectional diversities, gradually melted away, and a "common dialect" was acknowledged by all writers. The French wars, the extension of commerce, the contact between England and foreign climes, the cultivation of the civil law, all augmented the wealth of the vocabulary. Stimulated by these and similar agencies, the vocabulary increased very rapidly, so rapidly, that it is commented upon by the authors of that time. The language had now attained a condition which adapted it to the mighty instrument now brought to bear upon it, and destined to wield a determining influence in shaping its fortunes and directing its career.†

---

* During the Wars of the Roses, many of the Norman nobility perished on the scaffold, and many, expatriated, wandered in foreign lands, begging their bread in those very regions from which their ancestors had set out to the field of Hastings.

† Changes in English between Chaucer and Caxton. A large class of Anglo-Saxon compounds perished, such as, to *out-come*, to *out-go*, to *in-come*, to *in-go*. Their places have been supplied by Latin terms, as *depart, enter;* to *before-come*, to *anticipate.—Wood.*

CHAPTER XVII.

THE INFLUENCE OF PRINTING UPON THE ENGLISH LANGUAGE.

The Wars of the Roses left the English language in a more uniform condition; they greatly simplified its structure, and introduced many important changes in pronunciation, some of which are exhibited in a preceding chapter (Chapter XIV). But notwithstanding their beneficial results, they were attended by disadvantages also. The language was rendered more generally intelligible; local and dialectic peculiarities were in great measure effaced in the blending and interfusion of races, and in the thorough reconstruction of society. But while the language in its transmuted state was more widely intelligible than any previous tongue or dialect, it was thoroughly crude and unregulated. It had attained uniformity and simplicity, but it lacked harmony and proportion. During the progress of the fierce and sanguinary struggle, the art of printing, invented in 1440, was introduced into England (1474) by Caxton, who established his press in the almonry of Westminster Abbey. This at first acted as a disturbing element, and tended to augment the existing disorder, though in the end it essentially promoted orthoëpical and orthographical consistency, uniformity of speech, and elegance in literary composition.

Caxton was a man of scholarly attainments, but the workmen whom he brought with him from the Continent were Dutchmen, who were versed merely in the mechanical part of their art, and not acquainted with the structure or the orthoëpy of the English tongue. Hence the immense advantages of printing were for some time imperfectly appreciated in England, and it failed to acquire that artistic excellence which it attained in other lands soon after its introduction.* In the Continental countries the printers were among the most accomplished scholars of the age, a fact which accounts for the perfection that the art there attained. The foreign handicraftsmen whom Caxton had brought to England resorted to numerous arbitrary devices, the clipping or contracting of syllables, the extension of words; in their ignorance of our orthoëpical system, they failed to distinguish words resembling each other in sound but differing in meaning, such as *eminent* and *imminent*,

---

* "The importance of the invention of printing, startling and mysterious as it seemed, was very imperfectly appreciated by contemporary Europe. It was at first regarded only as an economical improvement, and in England it was slow in producing effects which were much more speedily realized on the Continent. In England for a whole generation its influence was scarcely perceptible in the increase of literary activity, and it gave no sudden impulse to the study of the ancient tongues, though the printing-offices of Germany and Italy, and less abundantly of France, were teeming with editions of the Greek and Latin classics, as well as of the works of Gothic and Romance writers, both new and old. The press of Caxton was in active operation from 1474 to 1490. In these sixteen years it gave to the world sixty-three editions, among which there is not the text of a single work of classic antiquity. An edition of Terence, published in 1497, was the first classical work published in England. It does not appear that Caxton's press issued a single original work by a contemporary English author, if we except his own continuations of older works published by him."—*Marsh, Wood.*

*pres*ident and *prece*dent, ingeni*ous* and ingen*uous*. Every printer seems to have been guided by his phonetic appetencies, and the sanction of authority was thus impressed upon numerous anomalies and diversities of spelling. In addition, Caxton himself appears to have had no uniform standard, and it seems to have been his general practice to reduce the orthography of the authors that he printed to the usage of his own age, or rather to an arbitrary standard of his own devising. The early productions of the English press were, in great measure, translations from the French.* Caxton had spent many years in France, and his style is pervaded by Gallicisms both in vocabulary and in structure, and the number of French words and idioms introduced by him was very considerable. This was another cause of confusion and discrepancy.

The ultimate effects of printing, however, were beneficial in the extreme, and there can be no doubt that it is the most potent mechanical agency which has affected the fortunes of our tongue. Like all inventions, in its earlier stages it was liable to perversion and misapplication, but when its real character and importance were distinctly apprehended, it proved a most influential agent in dispelling the prevailing rudeness, in facilitating elegance and harmony of style, and in promoting uniformity and regularity of speech. The number of books and of readers was multiplied, the various dialects became more and more assimilated to the southern, or the speech of the capital and of the southern counties of the kingdom. Authors were enabled to address a larger

---

* Most worthy of commemoration among the works printed by Caxton, are Malorye's "Morte D'Arthur," printed in 1485, and the works of Chaucer, Gower, and Lydgate.

reading public than before; the dialect of books began gradually to extend its sway and to supplant local forms and provincial usages, except among the uneducated classes, to whom books were not accessible.

Printing also promoted many changes which it did not directly originate. The decay of inflections, and the consequent adoption of a syntactical structure, logical, not formal, in character, in which the relations of words are indicated, not by their terminations, but by the order of collocation or arrangement, necessitated essential changes in the construction of sentences. "It became necessary to divide into short and separate propositions, sentences which would otherwise have become involved and obscure, when nearly all the cases had but one form, and when the various persons of the verb had become almost entirely undistinguishable from each other." The complicated, periodic style which is intelligible in an inflected tongue, is impossible in an analytic language like the English, without obscuring the author's meaning, if not rendering it wholly unintelligible. Independent and subordinate sentences in English must necessarily have the same form, and hence the necessity in these and in similar cases for some artificial contrivance, some mechanical device, such as *pauses*, *stops*, etc., to indicate those changes in meaning, which, in an inflected tongue, are made sufficiently clear by the terminations. The comparative facility with which printing was read stimulated the tendency to supply artificial expedients, and this, in conjunction with the disposition to write as briefly as possible, to make the sentence a whole, to be apprehended by the mind at once, and not an assemblage of various words, to be grasped separately, required an additional use of marks to aid the eye and to separate the parts of sentences. · Hence, from the new conditions resulting from the invention of printing, arose, among other beneficial effects, the art of punctuation, which has materially simplified our grammar, as well as affected our modes of thought and our styles of composition.

CHAPTER XVIII.

THE ENGLISH LANGUAGE FROM THE COMMENCEMENT OF THE SIXTEENTH CENTURY TO THE ACCESSION OF ELIZABETH. 1500–1558.

BETWEEN the time of Caxton and the death of Henry VIII., 1547, our language underwent considerable improvement, in consequence of the introduction of printing and the more extended diffusion of knowledge. Many of its superfluous forms were cast off; many of its useless particles and prolix constructions were abandoned. The literary productions of that age manifest gradual progress and advancement; display greater brevity of expression, as well as compactness of construction, and even occasional elegance. But this improvement, beneficial as its effects were, was only partial, and much remained to be accomplished before the language could be divested of its ancient rudeness, its redundant forms, and its cumbrous idioms.

The most important philological and literary monument of the first quarter of the sixteenth century is Lord Berners's translation of the "Chronicles of Froissart," the first volume of which appeared in 1523, the second in 1525. The translation is executed with remarkable accuracy, and conforms so closely to the English idiom that it has the air of an original work. The orthography of the translation is irregular and confused, a defect which may be attributed to the foreign printers, who were ignorant of the orthoëpy and orthography of the English tongue.

Another literary production of the first half of this century, which is valuable in a philological as well as in an historical point of view, is the "Life of Richard III.," by Sir Thomas More, printed in 1543. The style of the work displays a more advanced phase of the language than Lord Berners's translation, or than any other secular prose of this period, and it is probably the first specimen of good English prose, "pure and conspicuous, well chosen, without vulgarisms or pedantry."

The most important production of this period, and the one which exerted a more decided influence upon English philology than any other native work between the ages of Chaucer and of Shakspere, is Tyndale's translation of the New Testament, first published in 1526. The English of Tyndale contrasts strangely with that of his contemporaries. While their style is characterized by awkward periphrases, and is modelled upon the involved and complicated periods of the Latin, that of Tyndale is thoroughly English in spirit and in construction, and represents a more advanced stage of the language than the secular prose of that age.

The same purity, or at least the same freedom from awkward and incongruous Latinisms, may be discovered in the writings of Latimer and some of the other reformers, though their style is occasionally rude and uncouth in the extreme.

It is in the admirable Liturgy of the Church of England that the impress of Cranmer's mind and heart is most perceptible, but the purity of his diction entitles him to exalted position among the writers of the Reformation, and to honourable commemoration in a history of the English tongue.

The sermons of Lever are pervaded by the fiery vigour of Luther, and they have been turned to good account by a brilliant historian of our own age.

Upon the capture of Constantinople by the Turks in 1453, the light of classical learning found its way to Italy, whence it was disseminated throughout the different countries of Europe. Upon its introduction into England, it was at first cultivated in accordance with correct and rational methods, and was restricted to the legitimate intention of transferring to the English tongue the elegance and the spirit, and not the *forms*, of the classic writers. Some of the most distinguished scholars were purists in sentiment, and Sir John Cheke, the illustrious Greek professor at Cambridge, formed a plan for the elimination from the vocabulary of all words not of Saxon origin. But these endeavours for the reformation of the language produced no perceptible results, and the first decided effects of the study of classical learning in England were similar to those that immediately followed the introduction of printing—additional confusion, discordance, and diversity. The cultivation of the ancient literature was speedily carried beyond its proper sphere. The votaries of classic learning, not content with transferring the graces of antiquity to the native tongue, aspired also to engraft its forms and idioms upon its structure. The result was awkwardness and incongruity unsurpassed. The language was oppressed with perverted imitations of classic graces, which sat strangely upon it; the free and natural English construction, simplified by the rejection of nearly all grammatical inflections, was distorted and burdened with the complicated syntax of the ancients; numerous terms, based upon Latin roots, ostentatious and pedantic in form as well as in meaning, were fabricated; the language appeared stiff, ungainly, and ill at ease, in its novel and grotesque habiliments.

These disastrous consequences of the abuses of classical learning were stimulated by the immediate literary effects of the Reformation, which followed in the train of printing, and the revival of ancient literature. It is a prevalent, though a mistaken, impression, that the Reformation was beneficial to literature and sound learning in the periods immediately succeeding.* On the contrary, it co-operated with the agencies already at work in marring the character and the constitution of the language. It provoked theological controversy, which was often conducted with acrimonious virulence; it narrowed the sphere of intellectual pursuits, and intensified the feelings of the combatants; it concentrated the abilities of scholars upon the all-absorbing themes of polemical and religious discussion. In addition to these causes, the standard of theological education in England at the outbreak of the Reformation was extremely low, and there were consequently few scholars of sufficient attainments to conduct a controversy involving such momentous issues. Hence, a recourse to Continental scholars was necessary, and the want of native learning and controversial skill were supplied in great measure from foreign sources. These, writing in Latin, introduced a specially Latinized phraseology, which naturally tended to augment the existing confusion. It was thus unpro-

---

* *Southern Review,* Oct., 1872. "Craik's English Language and Literature," Vol. I.

pitious to elegant literature; it imported numbers of foreign terms and phrases, ancient and modern, and "rendered zeal and confidence much more effectual aids to authorship than art or the graces of art."*

But the causes of confusion and disorganization are not yet fully specified. The Reformation in England induced a partial acquaintance with the treatises and the language of the German reformers; it led to numerous translations from the French and Italian, as well as from the contemporaneous Latin. The wars between Charles V. and Francis I., of France, the relations which England sustained to those wars, invited the cultivation of foreign languages and literatures, and especially of the brilliant literature which had been developed under the auspicious skies of Italy.† Then followed the fashionable affectation of Italian idioms and phrases, of Italian manners and graces, which prevailed so extensively during the earlier years of Elizabeth's reign and during the reign of her father. Italian novels and romances were the favourite diversion of the fashionable and refined; to understand Italian was an indispensable accomplishment among courtiers and nobles. England became "Italianated" in speech and in morals. The extent to which these foreign influences were carried in the earlier part of Elizabeth's reign may be inferred from Roger Ascham's energetic and repeated protests, from many allusions in Lily's "*Euphues*," and from frequent references in the writings of contemporary or nearly contemporary authors. The product that was evolved by the combined action of so many diverse and powerful

---

* *Southern Review*, Oct., 1872. "Craik's English Language and Literature," Vol. I.

† *Southern Review*, Oct., 1872.

agencies upon a language in a state of disintegration must have been a "strange medley" indeed.

The "strange medley," too, was enriched by vast accessions of materials, gathered from under the four corners of the heavens; the chivalric love of adventure, the development of commercial enterprise, the extension of geographical knowledge, the introduction of names for the articles, products, and commodities imported from many foreign climes, all tended to augment the vocabulary by the infusion of an enormous wealth of words. To cite one example: it is said "that the vocabulary of Philemon Holland's translation of Pliny has never been precisely ascertained." Such was the general condition of the English tongue at the time that Elizabeth ascended the throne. Its vocabulary was rich, copious, and varied, but heterogeneous and unascertained; the grammar was rude and unregulated, the syntactical order awkward, the pronunciation unsettled, its metrical principles and combinations undetermined. The vernacular tongue was held in low repute; its future greatness was unforeseen, and it was but little resorted to for literary purposes. The language, notwithstanding its amazing verbal wealth, was thoroughly disorganized, and imperatively demanded an entire reformation and reconstruction. It is true that during the latter years of Henry VIII., Surrey and Wyatt introduced *blank verse* into English poetry, a form of versification derived from Italian models.* This new unrhymed verse ripened

---

* Perhaps from Cardinal Hippolito's translation of Virgil's Æneid, which was probably the earliest specimen of blank verse in the Italian language. It is supposed, however, by Prof. Henry Morley, that the translation was made by the poet Francesco Maria Molza, "who allowed the cardinal to take the credit of it."

into perfection at a subsequent era, but it exerted at the first little influence upon the tongue; in fact, the blank verse of Surrey and Wyatt is scarcely more than prose.

During this period, also, was introduced by Sir Thomas Wyatt, the sonnet, invented in Italy by Vinea, in the reign of Henry III. of England, and immortalized by the genius of Petrarch. The English language is peculiarly unfavourable to the development of the special beauties of this graceful and difficult form of verse composition, but it has been cultivated with success by some of the greatest masters of English poetry, among whom may be mentioned Shakspere, Milton, and Wordsworth. The popular element in poetry, represented by the vigourous rhymes of Skelton, and the courtly element, represented by the Italian graces of Surrey and Wyatt, reappear in the luxuriant richness of the Shaksperian drama.

Having traced the action of the multiform influences by which English was reduced to its lowly estate at the commencement of Elizabeth's reign, we must now consider that series of processes by which, in a comparatively short period, the language underwent a perfect transmutation, and became the appropriate vehicle of Spenser's fairy song and of the marvellous revelations of Shakspere.

CHAPTER XIX.

THE FORMATION OF ELIZABETHAN ENGLISH.

PERHAPS no language ever experienced more rapid improvement, and underwent a more thorough reconstruction, than English, during the first thirty years of Elizabeth's reign. Nobles, statesmen, knights, scholars, even royalty, engaged assiduously in the labour of reforming the native tongue. Every phase of literary effort was diligently explored; the laws of style were carefully defined; canons of versification were prescribed; the metrical capacities of the language were expanded; its rhyming words were collected for the convenience of versifiers, and in every department of intellectual exertion the utmost zeal and energy were displayed for the re-formation of the vernacular tongue. Sir Philip Sidney, Puttenham, Webbe, Meres, Mulcaster, Levin, Sackville, Marlowe, contributed efficaciously to the improvement of the language, and tended essentially to stimulate the genius and the enterprise of native authors.

Roger Ascham and Dr. Thomas Wilson are worthy of especial commemoration as the precursors of this school of linguistic reformers, and the former is entitled to a lofty position in the history of our tongue, as one of the founders of a cultivated English prose style. He was among the first to reject the use of foreign words and idioms, which had become so prevalent in the reign of Henry VIII., so that the authors of that day, "using strange words, as Latin, Italian, and French, do make all things dark and hard." He laboured with praiseworthy diligence to inculcate the formation of a pure English prose style, and to rescue the language from the neglect and indifference with which it was regarded by his contemporaries. His zealous advocacy of the claims of the native tongue, and especially of its superior adaptation to the purposes of prose composition, produced a marked improvement in the style of the period. So unfashionable had the literary application of English become, that Ascham prefaces his "Toxophilus" (1544) with an apology for employing it, "doubting not that he should be blamed for it."

Dr. Thomas Wilson, one of the oldest English philologists, published, in 1551, "The Rule of Reason, containing the Art of Logic, set forth in English," and in 1553, "The Art of Rhetoric, for all such as are studious of eloquence, set forth in English." The treatise of Wilson powerfully aided the cause which Ascham had been advocating, the cultivation of English prose by scholars. It evinces excellent discrimination, and it tended to clear the language of foreign phrases and pedantic affectations.

In 1565 appeared the first English tragedy (Gorboduc, or Ferrex and Porrex), in which the recently introduced blank verse of Surrey and Wyatt was employed. It was composed by Norton and Sackville, the latter of whom, in the Induction to his "Mirror for Magistrates," had proved himself the appropriate herald of Spenser's coming greatness.*

---

* It was first acted in 1561-1562, though not published until 1565.

Christopher Marlowe, our greatest dramatic poet before the time of Shakspere, contributed successfully to the establishing of blank verse as the recognized form of dramatic composition. Its progress, however, was very gradual, as is evident from the mixture in various proportions of rhyme, prose, and blank verse in the plays of Shakspere.

In 1570 appeared the "Rhyming Dictionary" of Peter Levin, a work designed to facilitate the labours of versifiers. The preface contains some valuable observations upon the language of his time.

In 1575 George Gascoigne published "Certain Notes of Instruction concerning the making of Verse or Rime in English." "The Steel Glass," published in 1576 by the same author, is the first specimen in our language of an extended poem not dramatic, written in blank verse.

In 1582 Richard Mulcaster wrote his "Elementary, which entreateth chiefly of the right writing of the English tongue." It is inferior to the "Schoolmaster" of Ascham, but it contributed materially to the progress of English philology, as it embodies many acute and discriminating observations upon the language.

In 1586 was published a "Discourse of English Poetry, together with the author's judgment concerning the Reformation of our English verse," by William Webbe. It is valuable on account of its delineations of English poets from Chaucer to his own day. The discourse was written in advocacy of the new system of hexameter verse, which had been introduced by Harvey in spite of violent opposition.

The writings of Sir Philip Sidney were not given to the world until after his death (1586). His "Arcadia" was published in 1590, his "Sonnets" in 1591, and his

"Apologie for Poetrie" and his "Defence of Poesy" in 1595. The "Arcadia" was written in 1580–1581; the "Defence" and the "Apologie" in 1581. Sidney's prose style is the most graceful that the language, up to that time, had produced, though it displays an excess of art rather than an unconstrained freedom, and is more euphuistic than that of Lyly. "Yet, notwithstanding all the conceits into which it frequently runs, and also some want of animation and variety, Sidney's is a wonderful style, always flexible, harmonious, and luminous, and on fit occasions rising to great stateliness and splendour." Sir Philip advocates the capacities of the English language for the highest purposes of literary composition, and it is a remarkable evidence of his linguistic discrimination that he was among the first of modern scholars to perceive the superiority of an uninflected grammatical structure and a logical syntax, over an inflected structure, and a syntax based upon the formal relations of words.

In 1586 appeared the first English Grammar, written by William Bullokar.

In 1589 John Rider published the first English Dictionary of Latin and English, and English and Latin.

By far the most valuable treatise in the province of criticism which appeared during the period of reconstruction was Puttenham's "Art of English Poesy," 1589. It is replete with instructive information respecting the language of the time, and lays down elaborate canons for the guidance of poets.

In 1598 Meres published his "Comparative Discourse of our English poets, with the Greek, Latin, and Italian poets," entitled "Palladis Tamia, or Wit's Treasury."

Under the influence of these critical writers, the vernacular tongue rapidly advanced, approved standards of composition and models of style now existed, the language cast off much of its former rudeness, while it retained much of its former vigour and flexibility. Its roughness was tempered by artistic graces, but its bounding spirit was not repressed by rigid prescription, nor its rhythmical flow checked by the enervating procedures of a purely artificial era.

But there were other influences, not yet enumerated, which tended to enrich the marvellous affluence of Elizabethan speech, and to complete the process of redintegration in the course of a single generation. We must first remember what has often been said of the learning and literary pretensions of the queen, and of the nobles and gentry of her court. Elizabeth herself was a scholar of decided merit, and her example was imitated by all who aspired to elegance of manner or admission into the courtly society of the age. The queen was acquainted with Greek, translated two of the orations of Isocrates, a play of Euripides, the "Hiero" of Zenophon, Sallust's "Jugurthine War," Horace's "Art of Poetry," Boëthius' "Consolations of Philosophy," a long chorus from Seneca, one of Cicero's Epistles, and one of Seneca's. She also wrote many Latin letters, and original English works in prose and poetry, and she spoke with fluency the Latin, French, Italian, and Spanish languages. "An impulse was thus communicated, a fashion was thus set, and dignity was conferred upon literature and scholarly pursuits. Admiration of the Greek and Latin, and the desire to rival or reproduce the triumphs of the French, and especially of the Italian, inspired frequent imitations. These dispositions cherished an eager diligence of translation, not simply or mainly to transfer the thought and substance of ancient and modern masterpieces to home use, but for the sake of domesticating acknowledged beauties, and of training the luxuriant redundance of the vernacular to the disciplined and decorous shape of artistic composition. Roger Ascham, in his 'Schoolmaster,' commenced in 1563, and published in 1570, strenuously commends the practice of translation for the acquisition of style, and for the correction of errors in the still unregulated tongue." Classical learning had become a fashionable mania, Latinisms were prevalent in the conversational dialect, the fashion of interlarding sentences with Latin phrases came generally into vogue, producing a sort of macaronic speech, which is ridiculed by Sidney with exquisite humour in the character of Rombus, and by Shakspere in the character of Holofernes.

By the year 1625, every classic author had been rendered intelligible through the medium of translations. The great diversity of translations, the wide range of topics which they comprehended, called into requisition all the varied powers of the tongue. It was enriched by copious accessions of Latin and Greek words, and by the resuscitation of many native vocables which had become obsolete in literary composition, or were restricted to dialectic usage. In fact, the most remarkable feature of these translations is not so much their specially Latinized dialect, as the great number of native words that they revived. The translation of Erasmus's "Paraphrase of the New Testament," executed by Nicholas Udall, author of the first English comedy, at the suggestion of Queen Catherine Parr, is clear and vigourous in style, abounding in English idioms, expressive colloquial phrases, and terse Saxon terms. Philemon Holland,

Master of the Coventry Grammar School, was an indefatigable translator of classic authors, and his versions, which fill five or six dense folios, contain a rich mine of native linguistic wealth. Not only this new literature, but new inventions and discoveries, new ideas and aspirations, all demanded new verbal forms for their adequate expression. These requisitions upon the energies of the speech were fully complied with, and in a short time the vocabulary of reflection became as rich as that of imagination.

Another way in which the speech was simplified was by the amount of controversy elicited by the Reformation—the extensive literature of attack and reply, of political dissertations and pamphlets. The issues involved in these discussions were of a popular character, and contributed to simplify the structure of the language, and to assign additional prominence to the Saxon element in its vocabulary.

Thus, every phase of the language was re-fashioned and re-organized in the space of about thirty years. Under the judicious precepts of Ascham and Wilson, prose, a species of literature always subsequent in the order of development to poetry,* gradually assumed a

---

* "There is a general law according to which, in all nations, metrical literature has preceded prose. Almost from the first hour that Englishmen expressed their feelings in song, or sought play for their imagination in tales, they chose their vernacular for that purpose; whereas, in those departments of literary exercise which the world had long recognized as the proper dominion of prose—the great business of record or of history in all its varieties, the noble work of speculation or philosophical thought on all subjects interesting to humanity, and to some extent, also, the work of social controversy and moral exhortation—Latin had all along been preferred to English. An English prose was indeed nobly disentangling itself.

loftier and a purer tone. But much of the prose composition of the Elizabethan age is coloured by a poetic glow, and it was not until a much later period that prose acquired its modern form and character. The canons of poetry had been diligently explored, the metrical capacities of the tongue had been tested, the forms of versification had been thoroughly discussed, blank verse was slowly winning its way to favour, the necessities of translation had recovered much of the buried wealth of the language, and had tempered its ancient rudeness by naturalizing the decorous graces of Greek and Roman art. The great era of the English tongue was about to dawn.

Any account of Elizabethan English would be necessarily imperfect without an explanation of one of its characteristic features—Euphuism. It is an important phenomenon in the history of the language, though its

---

As was natural, it had disentangled itself in the form and for the purposes of pulpit eloquence. Allowing for the precedents of a Wycliffe, a Chaucer, in some of his works, a Sir Thomas More, and the like, the first English prose style was that of the pulpit, after the Reformation. Then, in the Elizabethan age, towering above a host of chroniclers, pamphleteers, and polemical theologians, there had appeared a Sidney, a Hooker, a Raleigh, and a Bacon. After such men had appeared, and there had been exhibited in their writings the union of wealth and depth of matter with beauty and even gorgeousness of form, there could no longer be a definition of literature in which English prose should not be coördinate with English poetry. And yet, so much had still to be done before genius of all kinds could sufficiently master the new element, and make it plastic for all purposes (some of those included which poetry had hitherto believed to be her own), that in the schemes of our ablest literary historians, it is common to count but one period of English prose prior to the age of Dryden and the Restoration."—*Masson's Life of Milton*, Vol. I.

character and influence have been so often misconceived and misrepresented. Many have derived their impressions of euphuism from Sir Walter Scott's delineation of Sir Piercie Shafton in the "Monastery," which is not merely an exaggeration, but a ridiculous and unpardonable travesty. Euphuism was introduced into England from Italy during the earlier years of Elizabeth's reign, and brought to perfection in the hands of John Lyly, a dramatic poet of this era, in his two productions, "Euphues, the Anatomie of Wit," and "Euphues and his England." Lyly was merely a representative of the prevalent literary fashion, and he imparted to euphuism, when at its climax, a typical and polished form. Some of its distinctive peculiarities, together with its name, are to be traced to the influence of the Platonic philosophy in England during the reign of Henry VIII., an influence which came also from Italy. The skill of Queen Elizabeth in dexterous phrases, and her accomplishments as a linguist, favoured the growth of euphuism at her court. The frivolous character of James I. lowered the dignity, while it extended the sphere of literary affectation. The fervour of political and religious enthusiasm imparted to the conceited and pedantic style a glow of life and passion, in the days of Charles I. and the Commonwealth. Its influence upon the language of England continued during the rule of Cromwell, and much of the language of the Puritans was euphuism, inflamed with religious zeal, and acquiring a sombre hue from the gloomy fanaticism of the age. The success of Lyly's work was immense; he introduced a new English, and elegant and courtly dames, nobles, cavaliers, and scholars were his followers. The essential characteristics of euphuism were verbal antithesis, strange contrasts, a straining after effect, remote allusions, and incongruous combinations. In the ordinary conversation of society, it doubtless became an absurd jargon, but in the hands of Lyly, despite its characteristic faults, it attained an elegance and simplicity of form unknown in the prose literature of that era, and which strikingly foreshadow the graceful ease of the Addisonian age. In its purer types, as exhibited by Lyly, it was an essential simplification both of structure and vocabulary, an endeavour to inculcate the graces of style by practical illustration, a sort of "art teaching by example." Few of the writers of the Elizabethan period escape the fascination of the euphuistic style. Sidney, Spenser, and Shakspere all yield in a measure to its influence, and the style of Sidney is more euphuistic than that of Lyly. No sphere of literary effort was able to escape the contagion. It pervaded, in its extravagant forms, the discourses of Andrews, the poetry of Donne, and, at a later day, the style of Fuller. Our dramatic poetry, the most native portion of our literature, was least affected by its influence. Its impress is visible until the era of the Restoration, when it was supplanted by the French models then coming into repute.

Euphuism is not, however, a feature peculiar to the Elizabethan age, nor to any particular era of linguistic history; it is constantly reproducing itself in diverse forms and with varying degrees of virulence. The antithetical brilliance of Macaulay is merely "the euphuism of the elder day," and in the discourses of the modern sensational school of divines, we have a strange resuscitation of the incongruities and fantasies of euphuism, without the redeeming excellencies which it attained under the culture of the graceful Lyly and his associates.

CHAPTER XX.

ELIZABETHAN ENGLISH.*

FROM the contents of the preceding chapter, the student is enabled to understand the combination of influences by whose action the English tongue underwent, in a comparatively short period, an entire re-formation, and acquired that richness, flexibility, and vigour which pre-eminently characterize the English of the Elizabethan era.

Upon a superficial examination of Elizabethan English, it appears to present this striking contrast to the English of modern times—that in the former any irregularities whatever, either in the formation of words or the combination of them into sentences, are allowable. In the first place, almost any part of speech can be substituted for any other part of speech. An adverb can be used as a verb, "They *askance* their eyes;" as a noun, "The *backward* and abysm of time;" as an adjective, "A *seldom* pleasure." Any noun, adjective, or intransitive verb can be used as a transitive verb. You can "happy your friend," "malice your enemy," or "fall" an axe upon his neck. An adjective can be used as an adverb; you can speak and act "easy," "free;" or as a noun, and you can talk of "fair," instead of

---

* This chapter is principally condensed from Abbott's "Grammar of Shakspere."

"beauty," and a "pale," instead of a "paleness." Even the pronouns are subject to these metamorphoses. A "he" is used for a man, and a lady is described by a gentleman as "the fairest *she* he has yet beheld."* In the second place, we encounter every variety of apparent grammatical inaccuracy. *He* for *him*, *him* for *he*, *spoke* and *took* for *spoken* and *taken;* plural nominatives with singular verbs, relatives omitted where they are now considered essential, unnecessary antecedents employed: *shall* for *will*, *should* for *would*, *would* for *wish; to* omitted after *I ought;* inserted after *I durst;* double negatives, double comparatives and superlatives; "more braver," "most unkindest cut;" *such* followed by *which*, *that* by *as*, *as* used for *as if*, *that* for *so that;* some verbs used apparently with two nominatives, and some without any nominative at all. In addition, many words, especially prepositions and the infinitives of verbs, are used in a sense different from the modern; thus, "received of the most pious Edward," does not mean "*from* Edward," but "*by* Edward," and when Shakspere says that "the rich will not every hour survey his treasure *for* blunting the fine point of seldom pleasure," he does not mean "for the sake of," but "for fear of" blunting pleasure.

Upon a more diligent inspection, these seemingly hopeless discrepancies and anomalies can be reduced to several distinct heads.

The Elizabethan was a period of transition in the history of the English tongue. The enormous influx of new discoveries and new ideas, resulting from the condi-

---

* This usage continued until the eighteenth century. I have found an example in Steele (" Spectator," 492), "as agreeably as any *she* in England."

tions enumerated in the preceding chapters, demanded for their adequate expression numbers of new words, especially abstract terms. Then the revival of classical literature, the prevalence of translations from the ancient authors, suggested Latin and Greek words (but chiefly Latin) as their proper equivalents. The language thus received copious accessions of Latin and Greek vocables. The involved and complicated periods of the ancients formed the models of Elizabethan authors. In the endeavour to assimilate English to the Latin syntax, the constructive power of the latter was strained to the fullest tension. But the influence of the classical languages acted principally upon single words and upon the rhythm of the sentence. The syntax was mostly English, both in its origin and its development, and several constructions that are considered anomalous (double negative, double comparative) have had from the earliest period an independent existence in English, and many of the anomalies specified above have their origin in some peculiarities of early English, modified by the transitional Elizabethan period. Above all, it must be borne in mind that early English was far richer in inflections than Elizabethan English. So far as English inflections are concerned, the Elizabethan period tended rather to destroy than to preserve. Naturally, therefore, while inflections were falling into disuse, various tentative experiments were resorted to; some inflections were rejected that have since been reinstated, and others were retained that have since been discarded. In other instances in which inflections had been preserved, their original significance had disappeared, and in other cases the memory of inflections that had been lost still affected the manner of expression.

I. Inflections discarded but their power retained.—
Hence, "spoke" for "spoken," "rid" for "ridden,"
"you ought not walk" for "you ought not walk*en*" (the
old infinitive). The new infinitive "to walk," used in
its new meaning, and also sometimes retaining its old
gerundive signification. "To glad" (transitive), "to
mad" (transitive), for "to gladd*en*," "to madd*en*." The
adverbial *e* being discarded, an adjective appears to be
used as an adverb: "He raged more fierce."

II. Inflections retained with their old power.—The
subjunctive inflection frequently used to express a condition: "*Go* not my horse," for "*If* my horse *go* not."
Hence, *as* with the subjunctive appears to be used for *as
if*, *and* for *and if*, *but* (in the sense of except) for *except if*. The plural in *en* very rarely. The plural in *es*
or *s* far more commonly. *His* used as the old genitive
of *he* for *of him*. *Me*, *him*, etc., used to represent other
cases besides the objective and the modern dative: "I
am appointed *him* to murder you."

III. Inflections retained, but their power diminished
or lost.—Thus "*he*" for "*him*," "*him*" for "*he*," "*I*"
for "*me*," "*me*" for "*I*." In the same way the *s*,
which was the sign of the possessive case, though frequently retained, had so far lost its meaning that it was
sometimes (incorrectly) replaced by *his* and *her*.

IV. Other anomalies may be explained by reference
to the derivations of words and the idioms of early
English. Hence can be explained, *so* followed by *as*,
such followed by *which*, *that* followed by *as*, *who* followed by *he*, *the which* put for *which*, *shall* for *will*,
should for *would*, and *would* for *wish*.

These causes, however, do not sufficiently account for
all the anomalies of Elizabethan English. There are

several redundancies, and still more ellipses, which can only be explained as follows:

V. Clearness was preferred to grammatical correctness, and brevity both to correctness and clearness. Hence, it was common to arrange words in the order in which they came into the mind, with but slight attention to syntactical order, and the result was an energetic and perfectly clear sentence, though an ungrammatical one; as, "The prince that feeds great natures, they will sway him." As an example of brevity, "It costs more to get than to lose in a day."

VI. One great cause of the difference between Elizabethan and Victorian English is, that the latter has introduced what may be called the *division of labour*. This may be illustrated by a few examples. The Elizabethan subjunctive could be used, optatively; or to express a condition or a consequence of a condition; or to signify purpose, after "that." Now, all these different meanings are expressed by different auxiliaries: "*would* that," "*should* he come," "he *would* find," "that he *may* see," and the subjunctive form has become almost obsolete. "To walk" is now either a noun, or it denotes purpose, "in order to walk." In Elizabethan English *to* walk might also denote "*by* walking," "*as regards* walking," "*for* walking." In like manner Shakspere could write "*of* vantage" for "*from* vantage ground," "*of* mine honour" for "*on* my honour," "*of* purpose" for "*on* purpose," "*of* the city's cost" for "*at* the city's cost," "did I never speak *of* all that time" for "*during* all that time." Similarly, "by" has lost many of its varied powers, which have been transferred to "near," "in accordance with," "by reason of," "owing to." "But" has also yielded some of its rights to "unless" and "except." In the last place, "that," in early English the only relative, had been supplanted before the Elizabethan era in many idioms by "who" and "which," but it still retained its meanings of "because," "inasmuch as," and "when;" sometimes under the forms "for *that*," "in *that;*" sometimes without the prepositions. As a general rule, the tendency of the English language has been to divide the labour of expression as far as possible, by diminishing the task imposed upon overburdened words, and by assigning special shades of meaning to terms which expressed but one general idea. There are exceptions to this rule, as "who" and "which," but such has been the general tendency.

VII. The character of Elizabethan English is impressed upon its pronunciation, as well as upon its idioms and words. As a rule their pronunciation seems to have been more rapid than ours. The vowels were probably pronounced as in Latin, French, and German: The accent was fluctuating, owing to the contest between the native accentual tendencies of the speech, and the influence of the Latin accentual system. This will account for the varying and unsettled pronunciation of many words, which are accented sometimes on the first, sometimes on the last syllable. Hence we find *ac'cess*, and *acce'ss*, *pre'cept* and *prece'pt*, *in'stinct* and *insti'nct*, *re'lapse* and *rela'pse*, *com'merce* and *comme'rce*, *ob'durate* and *obdu'rate*, *con'trary* and *contra'ry*, *sep'ulchre* and *sepu'lchre*, etc. The conflict was adjusted by a compromise. Some words retained the Latin accent, as *respe'ct*, *rela'pse*: others were appropriated by the English, *as'pect*, *ac'cess*.

VIII. Words then used literally, are now used metaphorically, and *vice versa*. The effect of this is most perceptible in the altered sense of prepositions. For instance, "by," meaning, originally, "near," has supplanted "of" in the metaphorical sense of agency. With regard to Latin and Greek words it will generally be found that the Elizabethan writers use them in their literal or primitive sense: we use them metaphorically. This is evident from noticing the Latin words employed by the Translators of the Scriptures, by Shakspere, Bacon, Puttenham. Observe the altered sense of the following words of Latin derivation, occurring in the Authorized Version of the Scriptures, in Shakspere, and in Puttenham: *Censure*, to judge, simply, without regard to the character of the judgment: *convenient, consistent: conversation, acquaintance, association: denounce, to announce: insolent, unusual: offend, to cause to stumble, to entrap: officious, full of kindness: palpable, that which can be felt materially: virtue, manhood.* In the copious influx of Latin and Greek words into the vocabulary during this era, many were introduced to express ideas for which adequate provision had already been made in the existing vocabulary. These words, finding the ground they were designed to occupy already appropriated, were compelled to assume either special shades of meaning, or to adopt metaphorical, instead of literal significations. On the other hand, some Latin and Greek words that were used to express technicalities, have acquired a looser and more indefinite sense, as their original import has gradually faded away. Thus "influence" originally signified merely the supposed influence of the stars upon the fortunes of men; its meaning is now essentially altered. A corresponding change has taken place also in the meanings of "pomp," "ovation," "decimate."

The enumeration of the points of contrast between Elizabethan and Victorian English may seem to have been a mere list of anomalies and irregularities, and proofs of the inferiority of the former to the latter. But it should be remembered that the Elizabethan was a period of formation, of transition, and of experiment; and that its experiments were not always successful. While we have gained much in precision, elegance, and delicacy of expression, since the days of Elizabeth, we have sacrificed much of the ancient melody, the bounding rhythm, the nervous energy of our elder writers. It may be safely assumed, however, that the gains have compensated for the losses.*

---

* One of the most serious losses that our language has sustained, is the gradual decadence of the subjunctive inflection. Its judicious application constitutes one of the distinctive excellencies of our tongue, and it is employed with rare beauty and discrimination by our elder writers. It is one of those delicacies of expression for which the language furnishes no equivalent.

CHAPTER XXI.

THE ELIZABETHAN ERA. 1580–1625.

The student is now able to understand that combination of influences, by whose agency the tongue of England was transformed, redintegrated, and advanced to a degree of surpassing excellence in a comparatively brief period, so that to the unregulated, fluctuating speech which marked the early years of the Virgin Queen's reign, succeeded the fairy strains of Spenser, the verbal affluence of Shakspere, the stately periods of Hooker, the practical philosophy and far-reaching wisdom of Bacon's Essays. Lyly's "Euphues," 1579–1580, and Sidney's "Apology," 1580–1581, may be taken as the commencement of the Elizabethan era. Many of the noblest productions of this era belong, properly, not to the reign of Elizabeth, but to that of her successor, James I., to the seventeenth rather than to the sixteenth century. Still, the designation is a correct one: the excellence of the language was attained during her reign; its capabilities were developed and matured during this period, and its wonderful improvement was the result of causes which had their origin at that date, although they may not have produced their most brilliant results until the succeeding century

The Elizabethan era is not only the greatest in the history of the English language, but the greatest, perhaps, in the history of the world. Every phase of the language was called into action, all its latent energies were quickened, its manifold powers put forth all their strength. No department of literary effort failed to participate in the glorious awakening of the human mind. The Reformation and the Renaissance broke the thraldom of scholasticism, and led forth the intellect from the house of bondage. It was essentially an age of action, of enterprise, of lofty daring, and splendid achievement. The study of ancient literature, now pursued in conformity to rational methods, smoothed the ruggedness of our tongue, and adorned it with the graces of classic art. The process of dialectic regeneration contributed to the existing richness of the current speech, by drawing freely upon the ancient fountains of the language, and calling into requisition its varied and exuberant resources. Dialectic forms are used without reserve by the dramatists of the Elizabethan era, and it constitutes one of the great periods of dialectic regeneration in the history of the English tongue. The language and the literature of the Elizabethan era are characterized by boldness, originality, vigour of expression, and the absence of those conventional restraints with which the critical taste of later ages has in great measure restricted the ancient freedom of our tongue. It is the great era of creative power and of original conception, when authors, unencumbered with a profusion of learning, and unfettered by the rigid prescriptions of subsequent criticism, surrendered themselves to the guidance of their own impulses, wrote as they felt, regarding more the substance than the form and texture of their compositions. Art and nature were harmoniously blended, though nature predominated; and genius, free from the enervating influences of an Augustan age, soared into the very heavens in its unfettered flights. Every department of intellectual effort was strained to the fullest tension; the drama, which attained its completed form about the middle of the sixteenth century, revealed to the uneducated classes the splendid creations of contemporary artists, and afforded them occasional glimpses of that incomparable literature, which was otherwise to them a book with seven seals. It thus tended to promote simplification of speech, and served as the connecting link between prose and verse. The process of transition may be traced in the plays of Shakspere, in which rhyme, prose, and blank verse are blended in varying proportions.

In the hands of Spenser,* the spirit of Chaucer awoke from its dreary slumber, touched as by an enchanter's wand. While Spenser cannot be ranked as the greatest of our poets, his poetry is the most musical in our language. So delicate and subtle is his perception of the connection between sound and sense, that one of the most accomplished philologists of the present age has cited his rhymes, in order to illustrate the action of the onamatopoetic or imitative principle in the development of speech.† His fairy strain rose "with no middle

---

* The influence of Chaucer upon the English language and literature of the latter half of the sixteenth century, appears to have been very decided, and is beginning to be investigated with the zeal and attention which its importance demands. Spenser's archaic diction is partly due to the influence of Chaucer; there are well-defined traces of his influence in the plays of Shakspere, especially in "Troilus and Cressida;" and there are numerous allusions to the great poet in the literature of that era, in Ben Jonson, Daniel, Drayton, etc.

† Introduction to Wedgewood's "Etymological Dictionary," 1st edition.

flight" into the poetic firmament; every word is a lucid crystallization of the thought, every sound a clear, ringing echo of the sense. The influence of Spenser's poetry, in refining and expanding the metrical forms and capabilities of our tongue, as well as his influence upon succeeding generations of poets, cannot be too highly estimated. Under his guidance, our poetry attained the full consciousness of its powers. England was now a land of song, and the most productive period of our poetical literature had fairly commenced. But the "olde order changeth, yielding place to new;" a greater than Spenser was soon to appear; his conservative disposition and his retention of archaic forms and dialectic peculiarities excited unfavourable criticism, even during the Elizabethan era. The poet of chivalry, veiled in allegorical drapery, was to be succeeded by the poet of nature; and in our own time, the popular estimate of Spenser, like the popular estimate of Addison, is traditional, rather than critical.

"What are commonly called the minor poets of the Elizabethan age may be counted by hundreds, and few of them are altogether without merit. If they have nothing else, the least gifted of them have at least something of the spirit of that balmy morn, some tones caught from their greater contemporaries, some echoes of the spirit of music that filled the universal air. For the most part the minor Elizabethan poetry is remarkable for ingenuity and elaboration, often carried to the length of quaintness, both in thought and expression; but if there be more in it of art than of nature, the art is still that of a high school, and consists in something more than the mere disguising of prose in the dress of poetry. The writers are always in earnest with their nature or their art, and the poorest of them are always distinguished from mere prose by something more than the mere sound."

In the dramatic productions of Shakspere, the speech of England reached the full meridian of its splendour. Though not so highly esteemed in his own day as his sensational but brilliant contemporaries, Beaumont and Fletcher, his influence upon the language of succeeding generations can scarcely be estimated; he may be said to have created a new language, or, at least, to have created a language within a language. There is a Shaksperian dialect almost as clearly defined as the sacred dialect, and next to those peculiar forms and consecrated idioms in which the oracles of God have revealed themselves to the English-speaking world since the days of Wycliffe, none are so firmly engrafted upon our tongue, none have so thoroughly permeated its vocabulary and phraseology, as the inimitable combinations of Shakspere. His verbal affluence surpasses that of every other writer; his vocabulary* is as comprehensive and varied as his conceptions of humanity; it calls into requisition all the resources of that marvellous speech whose luxuriant richness had been gathered from the four quarters of the earth, which had been moulded and ascertained by the painstaking labours of a race of writers endowed with rare discrimination, and imbued with ardent zeal for the improvement and advancement of their mother tongue.

In the "Ecclesiastical Polity" of Hooker, the language of theology attained its loftiest excellence. His style is

---

* Shakspere employs fifteen thousand words, perhaps one-third of the vocabulary of English in that age.

Latinized, complicated, and sometimes obscure, but he is considered the first English prose writer, "that exhibits philosophical precision and uniformity in the use of words, and this is the peculiarity of his style which gives it its greatest philological value. This nicety of discrimination he extends even to particles."

In the style of Bacon's "Essays," we have an example of the speech of the most highly educated persons, in the conversational discussion of practical philosophy, exhibiting the excellences of euphuism, without its characteristic weaknesses. The style of the "Essays" is fascinating, though partaking somewhat of Elizabethan freedom and disregard of grammatical proprieties.

The final settlement of the Reformed religion, in the reign of Elizabeth, led to the establishment of the Liturgy of the Anglican Church, which in its various forms was prepared during the reigns of Edward VI. and Elizabeth. This unsurpassed manual of devotion, with its melodious rhythm, sonorous periods, and felicitous blending of Saxon and Romance synonyms, has powerfully affected the character of our speech, and enriched it with a variety of beautiful and impressive phraseological combinations.

Ben Jonson, the friend and contemporary of Shakspere, endeavoured to graft upon the English drama the forms of classic art; Terence and Seneca were the models to which he desired to assimilate the bounding spirit of the English tongue. But it is especially as a linguistic reformer that Jonson is entitled to the respect and gratitude of subsequent generations. His "English Grammar" was the first scientific and systematic treatise of the kind in the language, and its influence in defining and regulating the parts of speech was greater than that of any preceding or succeeding work. The distinguished consideration in which Jonson was held by his contemporaries, the deference and homage which were accorded to him in cultivated circles, gave him an almost dictatorial power, as the arbiter of speech. That he left a deep impression upon the English of his time, may be inferred from the eulogies bestowed upon his memory, in which he is represented as bringing the language from a state of confusion to melody and harmony. Some allowance must be made to the spirit of adulation in which such productions are generally conceived, but they are at least significant indications of the estimation in which Jonson was held as an expositor and a reformer of the vernacular tongue.

The time would fail us to speak of the dramatists, poets, divines, travellers, scholars, philosophers and historians, whose varied productions contributed to the glory of this brilliant era. It is the great central point upon which all the diversified powers of the language were concentrated; the perennial fountain from which flow rich streams of intellectual nutriment; and the period of our linguistic history which demands the most critical study, and the one that will most amply repay all the generous culture that may be bestowed upon it. The influence of the Elizabethan age is not bounded by the dominion of the English language; its light is gone out into all the nations, realizing, with historic verity, the far-reaching vision of the poet Daniel:

"And who, in time, knows whither we may vent
    The treasure of our tongue ? to what strange shores
 This gain of our best glory shall be sent,
    To enrich unknowing nations with our stores ?
What worlds in the yet unformed Occident,
    May come refined with accents that are ours ?

> Or who can tell, for what great work in hand,
>   The greatness of our style is now ordained ?
> What powers it shall bring in, what spirits command,
>   What thoughts let out, what humours keep restrained,
> What mischief it may powerfully withstand,
>   And what fair ends may thereby be attained ?" *

NOTE.—The possessive *its*.—It is during the Elizabethan era that the possessive form *its* first occurs in the written English language. It had probably existed long before in the current speech. It did not occur in the Authorized Version of the Scriptures, where *his*, *thereof*, supply its place, though it was subsequently interpolated (1653); Leviticus xxv. 5. It is found nine times in Shakspere, several times in Milton. The first example of its use is in Florio's "World of Words," 1598. The word passed through a variety of fortunes before its rights were generally conceded. The present use is the last of three distinct phases through which the language passed in regard to the word in about sixty years. First, "we have *his* serving for both masculine and neuter; secondly, we have *his* restricted to the masculine, and the neuter left with scarcely any recognized form at all; thirdly, we have the defect of the second stage remedied by the frank adoption of the heretofore rejected *its*." Sometimes the occasion for its employment is avoided altogether; especially is this the case in Shakspere. The very idea which we convey by the word *its* rarely occurs in his works, and it has been remarked that its adoption has changed not only our style of expression, but even our manner of thinking. *Its* appears to have been firmly established in the written speech by the time of the Restoration, 1660.

Our awkward participial construction, *is being done*, etc., has passed through a series of processes somewhat analogous to those of *its*; sometimes approved, but oftener repudiated; sometimes avoided, as was *its*, and its place supplied by *in process of*, it has steadily encroached, and is now, I fear, hopelessly engrafted upon the language.

---

* These lines of Daniel's were written before the English race had acquired an extended foothold in the Western world. We are " the heirs of this augury."

CHAPTER XXII.

THE TRANSLATION OF THE SCRIPTURES.

The Authorized Version of the Scriptures now in use among all English-speaking Protestants was executed by command of King James I. of England, being commenced in 1607 and completed and published in 1611. Its relations to the English language are more important than those of any other work, and no other European version, except perhaps that of Luther, has exercised so great an influence upon the character of the language to which it belongs. In the first place, the English people were more thoroughly imbued with the essential principles of the Reformation than any other European nation, and among them the Bible acquired a more extended circulation than in other lands. Again, the great theological and political issues which grew out of the Reformation, were protracted longer in England than elsewhere. From the year 1611, the present version of the Scriptures was appealed to as the supreme arbiter in all controverted religious and civil questions. From the accession of Elizabeth, but more especially from the accession of her successor, until the arbitrary enactments which characterized the earlier years of Charles II.'s reign suppressed for a time the religious liberties of England, the highest interests which affected man's welfare in this present life, and his happiness in that which is to come, were present to the mind of every reflecting Englishman as points to be determined at his own peril and by the light drawn from the inspired volume. Hence, it constituted a part of the intellectual and moral wealth of the English people, and it incorporated itself with their speech to a greater extent than any other book had ever done. Notwithstanding the objections urged against particular features of the translation by the advocates of either side in theological controversy, its excellence soon secured its general acceptance, and it has maintained, for two hundred and fifty years, the preëminence as the purest and most luminous exposition of the genius and beauty of our tongue.

It is a prevalent misapprehension that the English of the Authorized Version represents the actual condition of the speech as it existed in the reign of James I. On the contrary, it does not represent any particular phase of the language, or any definite period of its development, but it is a judicious and discriminating collection of all those forms of expression that are best adapted to the communication of religious truth which the language then contained, or which it had contained throughout the different stages of its history. We have learned that the dialect of Scripture is not subject to those essential changes of form and structure which have affected the secular speech. Its sacred idioms, its hallowed forms, seem to acquire, in a measure, the immutability of the truths which are treasured up in them. Hence, we discover that the dialect of Revelation has remained without essential modification, so that Wycliffe and Tyndale would recognize in our version principally an expansion and a recension of their own labours, and in reading the inspired volume we are listening almost to the same accents that were uttered by Tyndale three hundred and fifty years ago.

Wycliffe is to be regarded as the founder of our sacred dialect, while Tyndale imparted to it that finish and perfection which so admirably adapt it to the communication of spiritual truth. Above all others the genius and spirit of Tyndale are impressed upon our version, and its generic excellence is in large measure attributable to the thorough appreciation of the power and beauty of his own tongue which distinguished this truly great man, the most illustrious, and perhaps the most gifted, of the English reformers. The translators of 1611 contemplated merely a revision of the labours of their predecessors, and it is to be regretted that their excellent preface is so generally omitted. From this may readily be seen the extent of their indebtedness to preceding versions. "We never thought," say they, "that we should need to make a new translation, nor yet to make of a bad one a good one; but to make a good one better, or, out of many good ones, one principal good one, not to be excepted against. That hath been our endeavour, that our marke." Their translation embodied all the excellencies of previous versions, from Wycliffe's to the Bishop's Bible, which was in general use at the time that the translators of the Authorized Version entered upon their labours.

The most important changes which have taken place in the language of the Scriptures since 1611, are the following: many words of Latin derivation were then used in their primitive sense. Since that time they have assumed metaphorical or special significations. Such words are *convenient, conversation, describe, denounce, offend, instant, prevent.* Some native words and phrases have lost their original import, *e. g.*, " take no thought." Some archaic forms and ancient inflections are retained, " all to brake " (Judges ix. 53), broke entirely, all to pieces, *all to* is an intensive form. " Fell downe, and *all to* dasht herself for woe; "* hos*en*, hose (Daniel iii. 21). This inflection in *en*, according to Ben Jonson, disappeared in the time of Henry VIII. The possessive pronominal form, *its*, did not occur in the Translation of 1611. It was interpolated in 1653, Leviticus xxv. 5. Of it; thereof, *his* are substituted. The form " its " is first found in the written language in 1598—Florio's " World of Words." The old infinitive prefix *for to*, occurs in several places, "*for to see*," " for to be done: " also the participial noun with the preposition *a* (at); " the ark was *a* preparing," " the people fell *a* lusting." The adverb is used for the adjective: " thine often infirmities," where we would now write frequent or many infirmities. This accords with Elizabethan usage. Compare Shakspere, " seldom pleasure." The pluperfect indicative is used with the force of the pluperfect potential. " I had fainted (I would have fainted) unless I had believed to see the goodness of the Lord in the land of the living." Some words occur which are now obsolete,†*ear*, to plough; (arare), Genesis xlv. 6, Deuteronomy xxi. 4; *wist, wot*, etc. Dialectic terms are sometimes employed: *fat* for *vat*, Joel iii. 13.

---

* Sackville's Induction.

† The number of words in the Bible, which are now obsolete, or which are used in the United States with meanings different from those that they formerly had, is estimated by Marsh at two hundred and fifty. In the Old Testament, five thousand six hundred and forty two words are employed.

CHAPTER XXIII.

THE CHANGES IN THE ENGLISH LANGUAGE SINCE THE ELIZABETHAN ERA.

During the Elizabethan era, the English language acquired a degree of stability which it had never attained in the previous ages of its history. Its latent capabilities were developed, and its varied powers were perfected by the most splendid culture that has ever been bestowed upon any speech. Its mutations in the succeeding periods have not been so violent nor so essential as those which preceded the age of Elizabeth. But as language is the most sympathetic of all the productions of the human mind, reflecting with unerring accuracy the fortunes of those who use it, and receiving a deep impression from the peculiar conditions, and the new relations, introduced by each succeeding era in its history, so every speech is liable to changes, in vocabulary, in style, and in pronunciation. It possesses a power of adjustment, a faculty of adaptation to the demands which are made upon its resources, by the extension of mechanical pursuits, the diffusion of scientific knowledge, the rise of artistic tastes, the progress of invention and discovery. Hence every language is subject to perpetual change and fluctuation. The language of Shakspere and Ben Jonson would be inadequate for the purposes of our complex civilization; the vocabulary of the present day would be in great measure unintelligible to Sidney, Spenser, or Bacon.

The changes in the English tongue since the days of Elizabeth are such as would naturally be produced by the altered relations and the new conditions of society, during the course of two hundred and fifty years. The most potent agencies of change have been the vast extension of commercial and maritime enterprise, the growth of mechanical pursuits, and the consequent increase of mechanical appliances, the rise of the physical sciences, each of which has brought with it its special nomenclature, the development and cultivation of æsthetic tastes, the wonderful expansion of human ingenuity in every department of scientific effort, the multiplication of domestic comforts, the advance of social graces and refinements, contact and association with foreign nations, foreign wars, conquest, and colonization.

From the combined action of so many causes, the vocabulary of the English language has been more than doubled since the Elizabethan era. In the days of Shakspere, the written speech probably did not contain more than forty thousand or forty-five thousand words. Our largest dictionaries, as Webster's and Worcester's, have more than one hundred thousand. *

In addition to the changes in the vocabulary, there have been important alterations in the styles of composition, in the signification and accentuation of words. In Elizabethan times, the involved and complicated sentences of the Romans constituted the favourite model of

---

* This estimate does not include our provincialisms, slang phrases, and local forms, which are part of the language, though excluded from the written speech. They may be estimated at many thousands.

authors. But notwithstanding their long periods, they used as few words as possible; conciseness and brevity of expression were sometimes carried so far as almost to produce obscurity. In modern times this process is reversed; we have shorter and more compact sentences than the Elizabethan writers, but we employ more words than they. Words of Latin and Greek derivation then retained their primitive signification. They have either passed over into metaphorical senses, or have been appropriated to the expression of special shades of meaning. In the conception of the Elizabethans there existed a closer connection between the *word* and the *thing*, than in later ages. The materialistic or realistic element was then much more powerful; since that time the language has become more symbolic and spiritual. Many words which were then in perfectly good repute, have become obsolete, or have descended to provincial usage.*
This may be illustrated by comparing the provincialisms of America with the English of the Elizabethan age. Our accentual system has been essentially modi-

---

* Notice the following list of words, which were at different periods reputable linguistic citizens. Having failed to keep pace with the general movement of the tongue, they have been passed by, and left to linger in remote localities, and among the humble and uneducated, who most zealously preserve the memories, the usages, and the accents of the past. Most of our provincialisms can be traced to the retention of ancient usage.

Argufy, for argue; *allers*, for always; *crap*, for crop; *belike*, perhaps; *blubber*, to weep; Beaumont and Fletcher, and by Spenser; *beant*, be not; *afeard*, once as common as afraid; *ax*, for ask, used by Chaucer, Gower, Wycliffe, and Tyndale; *bin*, for been; *a few broth*; *busted*, for burst; *clodhopper*; *fout* for fought; *hadnt ought*; *haint*; *het*, for heat; *mo* and *moe*, for more, Chaucer, Spenser, Shakspere; *mought*, for might and must; used by Palgrave and Lydgate; *hit*, for it, the common neuter of the A. S. personal pro-

fied. The Gothic constituents of the language have vigourously asserted their rights, and the tendency to throw the accent as far as possible *from* the end of the word is constantly gaining ground. The insular peculiarities of English have displayed themselves very strikingly in the pronunciation, which has lost, since the Elizabethan era, nearly all points of resemblance to the pronunciation of the kindred tongues, French, German.* The individuality and self-sustaining energy of the tongue have greatly increased. Many characteristic and ancient forms have disappeared; the weak or regular verbs have made constant encroachments upon the strong or irregular form, and many of our most useful and expressive Saxon preterites have become obsolete. This will be obvious to every reader of the English Bible, in which the old preterites are of frequent occurrence; *spake*, *brake*, *slang*, etc. The process had commenced, however, long before Elizabethan times; as early as the Anglo-Saxon period, nearly every verb introduced into the language from foreign sources, takes the weak inflection. This process commenced at a much earlier period. The parts of speech are now thoroughly ascertained and regulated; then they were fluctuating and

---

noun he; *think*, for thing; *jawed*, scolded; *cotched*, caught; *holp*, for help; *consarn*, concern; *his'n;* *riz*, for rose; *knowed as how; snub; gull; dumpish*.

Many "Americanisms," falsely so called, may be similarly explained. They are merely words and phrases that have been perpetuated by the descendants of the English colonists in America, and in their day they were as reputable and as serviceable as those which have supplanted them.

* In some portions of the United States, the orthoepy of the Elizabethan age is partially retained, as in Virginia, for example, where the broad Elizabethan *a* is often heard.

interchangeable. Conjunctions were then employed in profusion, giving to a sentence a stilted and constrained appearance. Now they are used less frequently, and with more discrimination. The language has been subjected to rigid grammatical discipline, and has gained much in the artistic graces of style; it has advanced in precision, refinement, and perspicuity, while it has sacrificed much of its ancient pictorial power, its pliancy, and its artless melody.

CHAPTER XXIV.

THE ENGLISH LANGUAGE FROM THE CLOSE OF THE ELIZABETHAN ERA TO THE RESTORATION, 1625–1660.

The Elizabethan era embraces the period extending from about 1580 to the death of James in 1625. No other era in history presents so splendid an array of brilliant names, illustrious in every department of linguistic effort. The light of this great age did not disappear, even in the comparative distraction and decadence that succeeded. So late as the middle of the Restoration, our higher literature preserved something of the spirit of the great dynasty which had passed away. Sir Thomas Browne, Jeremy Taylor, Cudworth, Cowley, Milton, the greatest masters of our language from the Restoration to the Revolution, were all born before the close of the reign of James I. and Charles I. The chief excellence of Elizabethan English, however, is properly to be referred to the period over which we have already passed. The reign of Charles I., it would seem, might have kept alive the spirit of the age which preceded it, and the achievements of the tongue might have been as illustrious as in the days of Elizabeth or James. Charles was a person of scholarly sympathies and exquisite tastes. The correctness of his judgment is manifested by his relish for the plays of Shakspere. But evil days were at hand. The political and religious discontents which had been repressed with difficulty in the preceding reigns now began to assume a formidable and well-defined character. The virulence of controversy, theological as well as political, began to divert the minds of men from the dignified and ennobling pursuits of literature. Poetry, affected by the prevailing tendencies of the time, was gradually divided into schools or sects. In some the spirit of Spenser was perpetuated, and with the Spenserians Milton seems to have been identified. Ben Jonson lingered until 1637, the last of the great Elizabethans, and the man who in his day most powerfully influenced the tastes and style of his countrymen. There was no longer an accredited oracle of poesy; Shakspere had been dead more than twenty years, Milton had not attained his thirtieth year. The polemical works of Milton have survived the test of time, and they are as truly Miltonic as his poetry. "As his poetry is unique in one portion of our language, so is his prose in another. It is prose of that old English, or as some might say, of that old Gothic kind, which was in use ere men had given their days and nights to the study of Addison, and when it seemed as lawful that prose should come in the form of a brimming flood, or even of a broken cataract, as in that of a trim and limpid rivulet." His style and syntax are thoroughly Latinized, and his vocabulary is pervaded by rare words of Latin coinage, used in their original import, and familiar only to the diligent student of our early literature. The earlier productions of his muse were perhaps the finest specimens of finished execution, artistic excellence, and exquisite discrimination in the selection and application of words, that the language had thus far produced. The crowning glory of his poetic career was reserved for the succeeding era, but the effusions of his youthful genius were not unworthy of the author of "Paradise Lost."

Poetry assumed a diversity of form and character; it reflected the sentiments of opposing factions, and the political and religious affinities of the author. We have a profusion of verse, exhibiting a strange variety of styles, gay, luxuriant, austere, fantastic, classical, and native. In poetry, as in religion, the period under consideration appears to have been the golden age of contrariety and diversity. The unsurpassed ballad of Suckling, and the graceful classicism of the English " Anacreon," are found side by side with the devout strains of Herbert, the pure and limpid diction of Wither, and the dreamy allegory of the "Purple Island." The relations of England to France, brought about by the marriage of Charles I. to a French princess, led to the partial imitation of French models, and introduced some of that neatness and polished correctness which peculiarly distinguish the productions of French art. This served to abate the extravagance of euphuism, which continued to infect our prose and poetry.

The greater part of the prose written during the first half of the seventeenth century was theological or political. The controversies of Charles I.'s reign, respecting the nature and constitution of the Church, displayed a range and depth of theological and ecclesiastical erudition which succeeding ages have never surpassed, perhaps never equalled. The Confession of the Westminster Assembly (1643 to 1648-9) conclusively demonstrates that in all the loftier attributes of theological composition, the language had lost none of that vigour and energy of expression which it had acquired under the culture of Tyndale and Hooker.

Much of the literature of this age is in pamphlet form,* and is marred by the resentments and acrimonies which are generated by civil dissensions and partisan strife. Hence, it discouraged the growth of refined composition, and rendered "zeal and confidence much more effectual aids to success than art or the graces of art." The popular element in the speech began to make its way into the written language; provincialisms more frequently occur, and the distracted condition of the nation is reflected in the deliquescent state of the tongue. The theatres were closed by order of the Long Parliament, and all dramatic amusements were rigourously proscribed by the zealous sectaries of Cromwell. Fanaticism and austerity did not fail to leave their colouring upon the current speech.† It is seen in the adoption of Old Testament phraseology and its common occurrence in daily usage: in the nasal tone, the sanctimonious drawl, which characterized the adherents of Cromwell.

The reign of Charles, and the period of the Commonwealth and the Protectorate, notwithstanding their pernicious tendencies, in some respects, produced beneficial results. The war of "broadsides" and tracts enlisted the interests of the masses; the topics which they dis-

---

* This was the great age of pamphlet literature in England; nearly thirty thousand were published between the close of the year 1640 and the Restoration, 1660.

† "During the usurpation (of Cromwell), such an infusion of enthusiastic jargon prevailed in every writing as was not shaken off in many years after."—*Swift's Works, Vol. IX., p.* 349.

cussed had direct reference to their political and social welfare; their style was simple, though devoid of elegance, and they possessed the elements of popularity without the forms and attractions of art. Their general dissemination must have affected very sensibly the structure of the language, by producing greater simplicity of style and departing somewhat from the complicated sentences that distinguished the prose compositions of that age. The process of simplification was facilitated by the civil wars, the commingling of men of different social grades and various degrees of intelligence, representing sections, still comparatively isolated and exhibiting marked differences of speech.

The era under consideration thus served to prepare the way for the more modern and concise style of writing that grew up during the Restoration, and which ultimately supplanted the sonorous periods of Taylor, Milton, and Clarendon.

CHAPTER XXV.

THE ENGLISH LANGUAGE DURING THE RESTORATION.— 1660–1685.

The events that were in progress during the period whose history we have been considering, facilitated the introduction of greater changes in the language, that occurred during the reign of Charles II. The era of the Restoration was a period of severe trial to the language of England, as well as a period of important changes in the structure of the speech and in the style and manner of composition. It is during this era that we trace the beginning of the modern and concise style of prose writing which in the end succeeded the Latinized periods that constituted the favourite model of Elizabethan times. This new mode of composition, which was developed during the reign of Charles II., was in the succeeding age remodelled, and invested with a purer character, by the diligent labours of Addison and Steele. Hence the Restoration marks an important epoch in our linguistic history—the commencement of its modern form.

But this result was not accomplished without a season of adversity, through which the language was obliged to pass in consequence of the political and social conditions of the age. Notwithstanding the comparatively distracted condition of our prose and poetry during the preceding era, they had, at least in spirit and in style, been native and idiomatic. They were the product of English genius, not repressed, but only modified, by alien influences.

But there was a serious change in this respect. Charles II. returned to govern a people with whose tastes he had no sympathy, and of whose literature he had no appreciation. His foreign converse had rendered him in disposition and literary predilection a Frenchman. His court was tainted with the levity and frivolity of French manners, and addicted to the usages and customs acquired by long residence in foreign lands. Rhyme was introduced into plays to gratify the French tastes of Charles, and thus a fatal blow was inflicted upon the English drama, then just beginning to recover from the austere tyranny of Puritanism. Under the influence of Rochester, Otway, Sedley, Lee, Etherege, Wycherley, dramatic, as well as other poetry, descended to a degree of depravity which has consigned much of it to oblivion, notwithstanding the pathetic power and constructive skill which it occasionally displays. The drama of the Restoration attained its height in Dryden, who sacrificed the nobler powers of his intellect to the prevailing licentiousness that had affected the more fashionable and polished classes of society. The national taste was vicious to the last degree. The masterpieces of Elizabethan eloquence and poetry were consigned to the tranquil slumbers of the upper shelf. Their style was crude and antique, the vocabulary uncouth and obsolete. The reading public of that age felt themselves separated from the language of Spenser and

Shakspere, by a wider gulf than that which divides the educated Englishman from Langlande or Chaucer. This may be inferred from the modernizations of Chaucer by Dryden, from various passages in his writings, and from frequent notices of Shakspere's plays in the diary of Pepys.

A new condition of society introduced a new manner of thinking and an altered style of writing. The stateliness of ancient ceremonial, and the dignity of ancient manners, faded away amid the laxity and frivolity that were dominant at the court of Charles II. These novel conditions of society could not fail to affect very sensibly the character and constitution of the language. The gay cavaliers of the Restoration abjured everything in speech and in demeanour that savoured of Puritanical cant or sanctimonious phraseology. The prevalence of French tastes, and the attempted assimilation of manners and language to French models, coincided with the violent reaction against the sombre sway of Puritanism, and essentially facilitated its progress. From the combined action of these causes, we discover an altered style of conversation, and a new fashion of writing, which present a striking contrast to the biblical phraseology and the drawling accent of the Puritan, as well as a marked antithesis to the stately periods of Hooker, of Taylor, and Milton. We begin to trace the commencement of that process of abridgment, and abbreviation of words and syllables, that corruption of form, which distinguish the Restoration as one of the great epochs of phonetic decay in the history of the English tongue. Nor did these influences affect the structure of the speech alone. Words originally pure and elevated in their import assumed a noxious significance; the language acquired some of that malignity and virulence which we have already indicated as characteristic of the Norman era.

There are several most instructive passages in Swift (a writer who has left us many valuable reflections upon the language of his time) relating to this subject, which we introduce to illustrate the remarks just made in respect to the condition of the language during the Restoration. After speaking of the "enthusiastic jargon" which prevailed during the Commonwealth and Protectorate, he continues as follows: " To this succeeded the licentiousness which entered with the Restoration, and, from infecting our religion and morals, fell to corrupt our language, which last was not likely to be much improved by those who at this time made up the court of King Charles II., either such who had followed him in his banishment, or who had been altogether conversant in the dialect of those fanatical times; or young men who had been educated in the same country; so that the court, which used to be the standard of propriety and correctness of speech, was then, and I think has ever since continued, the worst school in England for that accomplishment. The consequence of this defect upon our language may appear from the plays and other compositions written for entertainment within fifty years past; filled with a succession of affected phrases and new, conceited words, either borrowed from the current style of the court, or from those who, under the character of men of wit and fashion, pretended to give the law. There is another set of men who have contributed very much to the spoiling of the English tongue, I mean the poets from the time of the Restoration. These gentlemen, although they could not but be sensible how much our language was already overstocked with monosyllables, yet to save time and pains introduced that barbarous custom of abbreviating words to fit them to the measure of their verses, and this they have frequently done so very injudiciously, as to form such harsh, unharmonious sounds, that none but a northern ear could endure; they have joined the most obdurate consonant with one intervening vowel, only to shorten a syllable; and their taste in time became so depraved, that what was at first a poetical license, not to be justified, they made their choice, alleging that the words, pronounced at length, sounded faint and languid. This was a pretence to take up the same custom in prose, so that most of the books we see now-a-days, are full of these manglings and abbreviations."

These "manglings" and "abbreviations," of which Swift speaks, probably grew up in gay and fashionable circles. Their general circulation in those classes of society which were the patrons of poets and dramatists, affords a sufficient explanation of their introduction into the written speech. In all these movements we may perceive the process of transition, from the complex syntactical structure of Elizabethan times, to the concise and rounded periods of Addison, the energetic and perspicuous diction of Steele. The Restoration was the era of transmutation from the language of the 16th and 17th centuries, to the distinctively modern form which it acquired during the earlier decades of the 18th. The phonetic corruption and disintegration to which the language was exposed during the reign of Charles II., resulted in the breaking down of the stately proportions of our speech; it experienced a revolution in form and character somewhat analogous to that which was accomplishing in the moral and intellectual constitution of the nation that spoke it. But in the midst of prevailing corruption the glory of the language was displayed in undimmed lustre in John Milton, who "constitutes an era by himself." It was during this period also, that Barrow produced his admirable sermons; Butler his "Hudibras," which has largely affected the character of current English; Bunyan his inimitable allegory, in which are exhibited, to the full extent, the resources and the richness of the Saxon element in our speech; and that Waller revived the echo of long-gone melodies by his additions to the plays of Beaumont and Fletcher. The brilliant triumphs of Congreve's dramatic genius belong to the succeeding era.

In his two grand Epics, Milton enriched our speech with the varied graces of classic art; he reveals the primitive import of many of the vocables derived from the treasuries of antiquity, and adorns our tongue with many felicitous embellishments drawn from the speech of Athens and of Rome. His blank verse rises to a climax that no other poet has attained; his syntactical order exhibits the loftiest excellence that can be reached by skilful collocation; if the order of arrangement is infringed, the spell of his poetry is broken, the charm vanishes, and it relapses into languid and monotonous prose. In him the spirit of Chaucer and of Spenser was kept alive; he was the lineal heir of that great dynasty of whom almost every memorial had fallen into oblivion.*

In the succeeding chapters we shall trace the process by which the novel and imperfect style that had sprung

---

* Milton employs about 8,000 words.

up under the auspices of a corrupt court, and under the influence of French models, was recast and made the basis of our present prose style by the wits and critics of Queen Anne's reign.*

---

* During the Restoration, the English language received many words from the French, also some from the Spanish, as *desperado, reformado,* etc.

CHAPTER XXVI.

THE ENGLISH LANGUAGE FROM THE CLOSE OF THE ERA OF THE RESTORATION TO THE ACCESSION OF QUEEN ANNE, 1685–1702.

NOTHING is more difficult than to define by precise chronological arrangement the fluctuations or mutations that characterize the history of every language. All such divisions must be to a certain extent arbitrary, as well as artificial. The most that can be accomplished, is to approximate with tolerable correctness to those almost impalpable boundaries, at which a language passes from one phase of existence into another, from its creative to its reflective stage, or from its synthetic to its analytic form.

The greater part of the period included in the century that extends from the Revolution of 1688 to the death of Dr. Johnson, is distinguished by the existence of certain predominant characteristics, that began to be developed in the language during the era of the Restoration. These distinctive traits continued until towards the closing decades of the eighteenth century, at times appearing in greater vigour and excellence than at others, and again existing side by side with other influences, but still manifesting their presence and their power during the greater portion of the period embraced within the limits of the present and the succeeding chapter. The comparative uniformity of character that is impressed upon this era of our linguistic history, has induced us to consider it as one period (comprehending, for convenience of treatment, two divisions), exhibiting in the main essentials a general resemblance, and at the same time redeemed from unvarying monotony by certain deviations from the principal channels through which the language and the literature flowed.

The period under review is designated by historians of our language and literature, as the critical, the artificial, or the reflective era, in order to distinguish it from the Elizabethan, which is the great epoch of creative or imaginative power. Such a transition is in perfect accordance with the natural development of all languages. Every literature, in its earliest phases, is distinguished by the absolute dominion of the creative or imaginative element. But as the luxuriant fancy of childhood gradually fades away before the austere realities of maturer years, so the sway of imagination yields to those calm and reflective faculties that are called into action when the gravity and earnestness of manhood succeed to the fervid glow of youthful enthusiasm. In the present instance, it becomes us to trace the special causes by whose action the language acquired the distinctive features that were impressed upon it during the critical or reflective age.

The Revolution of 1688 found the language of England in essentially the same condition in which the Restoration had left it; nor was it sufficient to extirpate the deep-seated taint that had infected almost every phase of our prose and poetry. But it ushered in the dawn of a salutary change, and it marks the development of that critical and regulative faculty beginning to manifest itself in the English mind, which, coinciding in spirit with powerful foreign influences, now brought to bear upon it, constituted, for about a century, a determining element in nearly all the linguistic productions of English genius.

We have seen that the effects of French influence upon our language during the Restoration tended to stimulate the prevailing corruption, to furnish new models of depravity, and to intensify the sentiment of revolt against everything that recalled the sway of the Commonwealth and the Protectorate. But with the advent of the Revolution we trace the beginning of a new era in the history of the English intellect, and a new era in the form and character of French influence. Let us endeavour to discover the mode in which these two tendencies, the one native, and the other foreign, coöperated and combined, so that by the influence of their united action, the critical age was developed and perfected.

In the first place, the Revolution is the period at which criticism first established itself as a modifying element in English politics and in English literature. The Revolution itself was a criticism and a settlement of constitutional issues, a manly and successful attempt to fix in precise terms and definite propositions, and to establish on a legal basis, the rights and liberties of England. In every phase of the nation's life, the action of the same critical principle is clearly discernible.* But in the character of the literature, it is most conspicuously exhibited, as may be illustrated by contrasting the two poets who may be regarded as the highest types of the creative or Elizabethan, and the critical or Revolution period. "This kind

---

* *North British Review*, March, 1869.

of index," says an admirable writer, "is peculiarly significant, because men of genius instinctively reflect, if they do not even anticipate, the foremost intellectual tendencies of their own time. In his early years, we find the fervid imagination of Shakspere, the type of this first period, engaged upon his Venus and Adonis; Pope, the type of the second period, in his teens reading Boileau, and enriching his Essay on Criticism with the treasures of literary wisdom, blended with the shrewd observations of his penetrating intellect. The creative age, the age of great and vigourous productions in prose and poetry, had passed away. Instead of these, critical editions of Shakspere and the other English poets were undertaken for the first time, as well as dissertations upon their beauties and defects, and critical theories of poetry and literature in general. It is true that these theories were often one-sided, superficial, and the rules prescribed for estimating the intellectual monarchs of the preceding age, utterly inadequate and even absurd. But it must be remembered, to the credit of the artificial age, that while its criticism is narrow, cold, and hypercritical, diligent effort was made to establish correct principles of judgment in every department of intellectual effort, and important results were attained in history, philosophy, and political science." *

The impulse communicated to the regulative or critical faculty by the Revolution, reflected itself in the character of the English language for nearly a century, and constitutes its determining and informing element. Thus we find that the critical restriction and refinement

---

North British Review, March, 1869.—Revolutions in the Queen's English.

of the language, its circumscription within some definite limit, was the dominant idea of English writers, from the days of Dryden, who witnessed its beginning, and who was an ardent advocate of the scheme, to the days of Dr. Samuel Johnson, who saw its close, and whose Dictionary, published in 1755, may be regarded as a partial realization of the plan.* All homely and simple

---

* One of the distinctive characteristics of the critical age is the utter inability of its authors and critics to appreciate the excellencies and the grandeur of the creative school. There are numerous allusions to Shakspere's plays in Pepys' Diary, in nearly all of which he speaks of them not merely with disparagement, but even with contempt. Addison did not include Shakspere in his enumeration of English poets, 1694 ; in 1721, Shakspere's Works were only in their fifth (5th) edition, and the copies of that edition published twelve years before were sufficient for the public taste. " Lucilius," says Gildon, " was the incorrect idol of Roman times ; Shakspere of ours." " There is not one," says another of his critics, " in all his works that can be excused by nature or by reason." " There is a meaning," says Rymer, " in the neighing of a horse ; in the growling of a mastiff there is a lively expression, and may I say, more humanity, than many times in the tragical flights of Shakspere." While Shakspere was at this low ebb, and was regarded by thousands of persons of taste and culture, as little more than an uncouth, uneducated genius, no less a person than Alexander Pope became his editor. Whatever may have been his qualifications for the task, no one could do more to secure for the great poet a wide circle of admirers and intelligent readers. But even when supported by the charm of Pope's name, the publication of his works was deemed a doubtful speculation. Only seven hundred and fifty copies were printed, and of these a part could not be sold until after a reduction of the price, from six guineas to sixteen shillings. It is probable that even this could not have been accomplished, had not Pope undertaken to edit them. His comments were confined principally to verbal criticism, characteristic of the spirit of his age. The comparatively low repute into which Shakspere had fallen, was owing in great measure to the prevalence of French influence, and the preference for French and classic models.

phraseology was to be excluded from the vocabulary of poetry. Serious poetry, argued the critics of that age, ought to reject such common and familiar terms as *man, woman, cup, coat, bed, wine,* and to substitute such elegant and delicately chosen expressions as *alcove, fair, goblet, purple, swain, tide, vest.* Dryden seems to have contemplated the establishment of a Central Academy, invested with dictatorial power, such as that which had polished the vocabulary and impoverished the resources of the French tongue, and we find that Swift addressed a letter to the Lord Treasurer, Oxford, suggesting that "as a member of the government he should take some means to ascertain and fix the language for ever, after such alterations are made in it as shall be thought requisite." It was not the design of Swift to exclude new words from the language, but to retain and preserve all such terms as should receive the sanction of the proposed Academy.

In all these movements we discern the action of the native genius, assuming a critical form, stimulated by French influence and coöperating harmoniously with it.

In 1673 Boileau (1636–1711) published his "Art of Poetry," which exerted an immediate influence upon the style of composition in England as well as in France. Boileau, the friend of Molière, was the first to attack directly that "*bel esprit*" which Molière had ridiculed. "He stood up boldly in defence of good sense." "Tout doit tendre au bon sens," he said. His writings mark the decline of Italian influence in France, from which some of her greatest writers had not been entirely exempt, while others were completely subjected to its sway. The style which Boileau assailed was that of the Précieuses and the grammarians, which was rapidly falling into disrepute, from its innate weakness. The power of his satire soon completed its destruction, and he was immediately acknowledged as the great oracle and expounder of the canons of literary criticism. It was to the classic models of Greek and Roman literature that Boileau and his school looked for exemplars of elegance and perfection; it was by their conformity to the writers of ancient Rome that the writers of France were to be judged. This was the "touchstone" by which all their productions were to be tested. Nor was this an ill-founded or arbitrary canon of criticism. It is from the Latin that the French tongue has inherited many of its excellencies, and the rigid adherence to rule, the logical consistency and precision, that distinguished the cultivated speech of Rome, are strikingly perpetuated in its Langue D'Oyl descendant. The example set by Boileau and his followers soon extended itself to England, where it coincided with those reflective and regulative faculties which the Revolution had called into action, and imparted a new stimulus to critical inquiry into literary styles and forms of composition.

Rapin, Bossu, Dacier, Fontenelle, who like Boileau, looked to the ancients as the great standard of taste and excellence, had their advocates and representatives in England. Horace's "Art of Poetry" was translated into verse by the Earl of Roscommon; it was imitated by Oldham; while Boileau's "Art of Poetry," translated by Sir William Soame, a friend of Dryden's, was not published until it had received many touches from the hand of Dryden, who, in the preface to his plays, had proved himself the first of English critics, the most thoroughly independent and English in spirit. Yet even he cites in the preface to his conversion of "Paradise Lost" into an opera, as authorities in literature, "the greatest in his age, Boileau and Rapin, the latter of which alone is sufficient, were all other critics lost, to teach anew the rules of writing." The influence of Boileau and his school thus became as potent in England as in France. The change in the character of literary composition is distinctly perceptible in the altered style of Dryden after his "*Annus Mirabilis.*"* (1667.) Before that time he had produced all his rhyming tragedies, in which he deliberately followed the worst French models; afterwards he produced his best plays, his satires, and his didactic poems. His play of "Tyrannic Love," was the last in which he adhered to the excesses and extravagancies of his French prototypes; the salutary influence of Boileau begins to manifest itself in the more elevated and dignified tone of his works.

But if Dryden was subject to the sway of Boileau during the latter part of his career,† his lineal successor, Pope, was under his dominion during the whole of his literary history, and he has been termed, not inaptly, the "viceroy" of Boileau in England. He was thoroughly imbued with the teachings of French criticism, and it was in great measure due to his influence that these teachings so deeply impressed themselves upon the character of English literature during the eighteenth century. In him are reflected all the excellencies and defects of the critical era; no man had a greater number of imitators, and his poetry was, by general consent, the highest standard of scrupulous accuracy and finished

---

* Morley's English Writers.

† During the earlier part of his literary career, Dryden was under the influence of the metaphysical school of poets, Donne and Cowley.

elegance, during the greater part of the eighteenth century. He was emphatically the representative of the artificial age, thoroughly in sympathy with its spirit, and the fitting exponent of its linguistic and intellectual tendencies.

But while the critical age may be dated from the Revolution of 1688, while its essential characteristics are impressed upon the literary productions of the English mind, until the later decades of the eighteenth century, it was during the reign of Queen Anne (1702–1714) that the distinctive features of the era attained their loftiest excellence. It was during this period that our literature acquired that centralized, conventional, and urban tone which characterized the contemporary literature of France; it was then that eloquence assumed its modern form, that De Foe, the father of our popular literature, and one of the greatest names in the history of our language, established his "Review,"* and that Steele, following the 'example of De Foe, founded that immortal series of periodicals which mark so important an epoch in our literary history, and whose influence upon our style of prose composition is perceptible in every sentence that we write. The true position and services of the refiners and critics of Anne's time, have often been misconceived and misinterpreted. The concise modern fashion of writing which had grown up during the Restoration, under the influences indicated in the preceding chapter, was tainted with the linguistic corruption which prevailed during that era.

---

* De Foe's "Review" was established in 1704, five years in advance of the "Tatler." His experiment probably suggested to Steele the plan of the "Tatler." De Foe founded our popular literature; Steele and Addison extended and improved it.

It is true that a pure and noble prose style was slowly disentangling itself. The cumbrous periods of the Elizabethans had given way, between the Restoration and the accession of Queen Anne, to a more concise style of writing, which, beginning with Cowley, the metaphysical poet, was perpetuated and improved by a succession of prose writers in whom we trace a gradual approximation to the characteristic excellencies of Addisonian times. Cowley, Barrow, Tillotson, Temple, Halifax, Dryden, South, Sprat, Locke, and Shaftesbury, were the worthy precursors of our Augustan age. The last of these was the immediate forerunner of Addison, and laboured zealously for the culture and advancement of the language. Perhaps no one in this era, before the appearance of Addison, exercised a more decided influence upon the fortunes of English letters. Notwithstanding the merits of these writers, the conciseness of Cowley, the elegant simplicity of Temple, the vigourous English of Dryden, and the classical graces of Shaftesbury, much remained to be accomplished. The language was still seriously defective in harmony and precision: laxity, carelessness, and disregard of idiomatic proprieties, marred the compositions of the best authors. The outlines of our present prose style had been sketched, but the process was incomplete, and there was need of much skillful elimination, delicate polishing, and critical expansion. The spoken language retained the grossness of the preceding era. The conversational dialect in vogue in fashionable circles must have been corrupt and licentious to a degree of which we can form no adequate conception. In the "Polite Conversations" of Swift, we have a correct portraiture, drawn by the hand of a master and a contemporary, of the colloquial style that dates from the Restoration, and which continued to prevail at the time that Addison and Steele commenced their noble labours for refining and improving the mother tongue. A careful reading of these "Conversations" will reveal the fact, that many of the delicate repartees and polished jests, current in the better circles of that era, have since not only been excluded from the speech of reputable society, but have descended to the lowest degree of provincial and vulgar usage.

Such was the general condition of the language at the commencement of the eighteenth century. Under the influence of Boileau, poetry had assumed a purer tone. This improvement in our poetic dialect was carried out to its perfection by Pope.

But the style of prose composition was essentially defective, and needed a thorough reconstruction before prose could attain its exalted position as a determining element in English literature. We shall now see how this reform was effected.

CHAPTER XXVII.

THE ENGLISH LANGUAGE FROM THE ACCESSION OF QUEEN ANNE TO THE DEATH OF DR. JOHNSON.—1702–1784.

THE age of Queen Anne was preëminently the era of the critical expansion and refinement of the English tongue. The critical tendencies which had been developed by the Revolution, and stimulated by the influence of Boileau, attained their perfection in the graces of Addison, and the fastidious elegance of Pope. Steele and Swift were less subject to foreign influence; they represent the native or popular element in our literature, at a time when the English mind was in a great degree controlled by external forces. They appear to have been thoroughly imbued with the spirit of our tongue, and while they did not ignore the graces of style, and were in some measure guided by the prevailing tendency of their age, they maintained, like their illustrious contemporary, De Foe, a truly English character, which is rarely exhibited in the pages of Addison. This is evident from Swift's zealous labours for the improvement of the language, from his "Letter to a Young Clergyman," his characteristic delineation of the linguistic corruptions that were current in his own day, his earnest endeavours to secure for the English language a recognized place in the system of education, and his appreciation of our elder literature,* which had fallen into disrepute since the Restoration. The same English traits are displayed in the nervous and idiomatic style of Steele, in his exposure of verbal corruption and phraseological abuses,† and his graceful employment of purely Elizabethan constructions.‡ It is in Steele and in Swift that we distinctly trace the movements of our tongue during the critical era, retaining its ancient freedom and pliancy, modified by exotic influences, though never yielding to their sway. It was Addison who was thoroughly subjected to French influence. In his continental tour he had seen Boileau and conversed with him, and during his entire career, he seems to have looked to the critics of France, and to the fountains of Greek and Roman genius, as the true sources of inspiration and of excellence.

Addison occupies the same position in regard to prose style, which has been accorded to Pope as the acknowledged model of poetic excellence. His influence over succeeding generations was so great "that any thing which tended to form his style, modified, through him, the writings of almost all his successors throughout the century. He seems to have possessed the marvelous faculty of taking the good and rejecting the bad from

---

* "The period wherein the English tongue received the greatest improvement, I take to commence with the reign of Queen Elizabeth, and to conclude with the great Rebellion in 1642." This was the "barbarous age" that produced "old Spenser," as Addison styles him in his college poem, 1694.

† *Tatler*, No. 12.

‡ *Spectator*, No. 492. "As agreeably as any *she* in England." This is purely Elizabethan. I do not think it occurs in Addison. It is one of those slight but unmistakable touches which reveal the true spirit of an author.

the works of his predecessors, and in him, the rough vigour of the old English writers was softened by the delicacy and refinement of the modern French school. In his pure and polished style, we see this influence exhibited in its best form."* His conformity to French models extended the reputation of his works across the channel, at a time when English literature was almost unknown beyond the limits of the island. Many distinguished foreigners were among the subscribers to his works. In his tragedy of Cato, he observed the unities of time and place which have bound up the French drama within circumscribed and arbitrary limits, thoroughly opposed to the free and natural spirit of the Elizabethan school. Hence he received from Voltaire (who denounced Shakspere as a barbarian genius) the glowing tribute, "Monsieur Addison is the first Englishman who has made a reasonable tragedy." This of the nation that had produced Hamlet, Lear, and Macbeth!

The impress of Addison upon the language of his age and of the succeeding age was deeper than that of his greater contemporaries, and for the reason that he was in perfect accord with the dominant spirit of the era. Idiomatic in style, polished and perspicuous in diction, he was assimilated in sentiment and in taste to the masterpieces of antiquity, and to the critical canons of Boileau. The incomparable literature of Elizabethan times failed to excite his sympathy or to arouse his admiration; he was devoid of appreciation of everything that could not be conformed to the standard of

---

* Woods' "Reciprocal Influence of English and French Literature in the XVIII. Century."

"good sense," and he undertook to bring Milton to the attention of his countrymen by comparing him to Homer and Virgil, a mark of deference to the spirit of his age.

In 1694, an undergraduate at Oxford, we find Addison, in a poem on English poets, written for a college friend, omitting the name of Shakspere, and speaking of Chaucer and Spenser in such terms as these:

> "Old age has rusted what the poet writ,
> Worn out his language, and obscured his wit,
> In vain he jests in his unpolished strain,
> And tries to make his readers laugh, in vain.
> Old Spenser next, warm with poetic rage,
> In ancient tales amused a barbarous age,
> But now the mystic tale that pleased of yore,
> Can charm an understanding age no more."

Nor do his attainments in English philology, his acquaintance with the historical development and the structural peculiarities of his native tongue, appear to have been of a higher order. Thus, we find him explaining the *'s* of the genitive or possessive case, as the "*his* or *her* of our ancestors," and writing "Ulysses his bow" for Ulysses's bow. Of the genitive sign *'s*, Ben Jonson, in the "barbarous age" that produced a Spenser and a Shakspere, had given a much more rational and satisfactory explanation.

Among all the men of this time, perhaps no one contributed more efficiently to the establishment of a chaste and polished style than Bolingbroke. His exalted position among scholars and statesmen, the charms of his conversation, and the readiness as well as the finish of his eloquence, must have rendered him a model that all cultured circles strove to imitate. It is said that his ordinary utterances and impromptu speeches possessed all the rhythmical harmony and "golden cadence" that belong to painfully wrought periods, and which most men acquire by the assiduous culture of a lifetime. His conversation or his writings were rarely marred, even by trifling blemishes, and in an age during which correctness was much sought after and but little understood, he must have wielded a decided influence in forming and regulating the conversational dialect, as well as the style of writing of his cultivated contemporaries.*

The English genius, modified but not repressed, is represented in Dryden, Steele, and Swift. In Pope, Addison, and Bolingbroke, we witness the action of the native mind subjected to the sway of classic models and foreign canons of criticism, but even in its servitude retaining something of the spirit of its original freedom. Wherein consists the excellence and the glory of these writers? Not in original or creative power, for of this, except Swift, they possessed but little, and they seem rather to have avoided anything that bordered upon the sublime or lofty. Not in the extent or variety of their learning, for their attainments were, with few exceptions, lacking in accuracy and comprehensiveness, and there appear in every issue of the *British Reviews* articles surpassing in extent and diversity of knowledge anything that ever emanated from the pen of Steele or Addison. Their true merit consists in this: not that they invented or constructed a new style, but that they adopted the mode of writing which had come into

---

* Some idea of Bolingbroke's popularity and influence as a writer may be formed from the fact that his contributions to the *Craftsman* gave that journal a circulation far exceeding that of the *Spectator*.

fashion during the Restoration, eliminated its offensive features, infused into it a purer tone, and impressed upon it the essential characteristics of our present prose composition. They banished, in great measure, phonetic corruption and obscenity from the colloquial dialect, and gradually dispelled that lingering connection which still subsisted in the public mind between purity and austerity, between virtue and fanaticism.

Such was the task that they accomplished, and they performed it thoroughly. Their vocabulary was culled with fastidious and painful diligence, homely words and phraseology were rejected, the more concise and polished Latin or Romance terms were preferred to their energetic Saxon equivalents, their periods were constructed with supreme regard to symmetry and harmonious arrangement; external grace, beauty of *form* were the highest excellence to which the critical taste aspired.

Let us not misconceive the true character of this era, nor be blinded to its imperfections by the traditional lustre which envelops the name of Addison. Let us not indulge the delusion that the critical taste resulted in the perfecting of style, either written or colloquial. The adverse testimonies are too numerous to admit impeachment.* The conversational dialect of this age was blemished by phonetic corruptions, marred by gross and widely prevailing profanity, and disfigured by affectations as grotesque as those which characterized the worst stages of euphuism. It was against these abuses that the powers of the critical school were, in a great measure, directed, and it is in these respects that their labours were attended with most salutary results. The conver-

---

* Swift, Steele.

sational style even of the educated was pervaded by inaccuracies of expression, and Dr. King (1685-1763), an illustrious scholar of the last century, informs us that in all his associations with the men of his generation, he had met but three who expressed themselves with such purity and elegance that their conversation, if committed to writing, would possess the attractions of a finished and cultivated style. These were Bishop Atterbury, Dr. Gower, Provost of Worcester College, and Dr. Sam. Johnson. No regard was paid to the systematic study of English in schools, no attention to the cultivation of pure English style; treatises on English grammar appear to have been almost unknown. Affectation of French phrases, introduced by the Continental wars, seems to have prevailed; the want of training in pulpit elocution was more common then even than now; pedantry, and the absence of "the least conception of a style," constituted the bane of the clergy; the absence of accuracy and fluency of expression was a distinguishing characteristic of the age.* Much of this internal disorder is veiled from our gaze by the time-honoured glory that is associated with the names of Addison and Pope, and by the delusive splendour that gilds the Augustan age of Anne. The reputation of this era rests principally upon its praiseworthy efforts to eradicate the linguistic corruptions of a preceding period, and in its placing upon a firm and enduring basis our present prose style. In these respects its influence has been productive of most beneficial results. But the entire era is marked by its adherence to conventional usages; its theory of language was conventional, its criticism

---

* *Spectator*, 353.   *Tatler*, 70, 165, 234.   Swift's "Letter to a Young Clergyman."   Dr. King's "Anecdotes of his own Time."

was often superficial and circumscribed by artificial limits. In the popular literature founded by De Foe, in the productions of the great English novelists, Richardson, Fielding, and Smollett, the bounding spirit of the English tongue and the unchecked vigour of the English mind are kept alive; in the notes of Thomson, the preluding strains of Goldsmith, the polished compositions of Gray, the glowing verses of Collins, the graceful periods of Hawkesworth, the revival of our ballad poetry by the publication of "Percy's Reliques," we have occasional intimations of the glory that was to be revealed. But these deviations from the main current of the literature did not at once arrest those peculiar tendencies which had been so deeply impressed upon it during the preceding era, and other agencies, more potent in their nature, and more efficient in their action, were to be called into service ere should be broken the magic spell with which Addison and Pope had bound our prose and poetry. No one, even of the great historical triumvirate of the eighteenth century, can be regarded as a model of pure English style, simple and unaffected, "elegant, but not ostentatious." The style of Hume is marred by Scotticisms; that of Robertson and Gibbon by a pompous diction and a Latinized phraseology. With the rise of Cowper, we have the first decided indication that the school of Dryden and Pope was hastening to its setting, and with the death of Dr. Johnson the dismal uniformity of conventionalism begins to be dispelled.

In the concluding chapter we shall briefly trace the action of those agencies by whose influence the spirit of Elizabethan times was revived in full vigour, and an epoch in our linguistic history ushered in which blended the excellencies of the creative school with the softer graces of a reflective age, producing a combination which almost rivalled the splendour of the Virgin Queen's brilliant reign.

CHAPTER XXVIII.

THE ENGLISH LANGUAGE FROM THE DEATH OF DR. SAMUEL JOHNSON (1784) TO THE CLOSE OF THE GEORGIAN ERA (1830).

THE death of Dr. Johnson marks an event of the greatest importance in our linguistic history. It was the end of dictatorship, and "King Samuel" has had no acknowledged successor upon the throne of English literature. But it foreshadowed an event of infinitely greater importance than the mere downfall of literary autocracy. No writer, perhaps, was ever more thoroughly the exponent of his age, the embodiment of its conventional spirit, and its deference to ancient precedent. No man ever wielded a more decided influence in moulding the style, and directing the intellectual efforts of his contemporaries, and his diction, generally pompous, turgid, and thoroughly Latinized,* was the acknowledged standard of excellence among the writers of his era, nor did it fail to affect the style of succeeding generations. The coldly classical tastes of Dr. Johnson, his diffident and cautious estimate of Shakspere, are too well known to require comment. Hence, when he fell, conventionalism lost its ablest and most influential champion. This event coincided with the development of those mighty

---

* Dr. Johnson's style was in great measure modelled upon that of Sir Thos. Browne, whose Latinisms are worthy of careful study.

political conflicts which were soon to transform the character of European society, annihilate ancient prescription, efface the vestiges of feudalism, create new modes of thought, new systems of philosophy, and dispel the dreary formality which had marked the intellectual creations of the eighteenth century.

Every literature derives its form and colouring from the spirit of the era which evokes it to life; it is "the artistic expression in words, of what men think and feel." The style of every age has its clearly defined characteristics, impressing upon it a strong individuality, and distinguishing it from the style of succeeding or preceding eras. Each of these peculiar styles is developed by certain political and social conditions, and moulded in accordance with the prevailing tastes of the period. There was a style created by the Reformation in the sixteenth century; there was another formed during the Restoration, and perfected during the age of Anne; this style was expanded, and invested with a nobler tone and character, by the stimulus which the French Revolution imparted to every phase of linguistic and literary effort. Convulsing the depths of European society, it undermined the barriers of venerable tradition, dispelling the accumulations of long established prejudices and absurd veneration for antiquity. Isolation and proscription began to fade away before the advent of generous tolerance, enlightened sympathy, increasing appreciation of the true ideal in art, and genuine appreciation of nature. The true standard of excellence was no longer sought in mere external grace, obsequious deference to ancient prototypes, and foreign models. The spirit and character of the nineteenth century are, in every essential respect, a revolt against the dominant principles and established traditions of the eighteenth, a perfect antithesis to its conventional and superficial tendencies, a return from the purely formal to the investigation of the inner life; from the form to the spirit, from the outward to the inward.

This distinguishing feature of the present century is conspicuously displayed in every manifestation of its intellectual life; in the marvellous expansion of the physical sciences, in the splendid developments of linguistic science, which is based in great measure upon the *internal* resemblances of speech, in the brilliant generalizations of Cuvier, and the discovery of Grimm's law, in all of which the application of the same principle is exhibited in its grandeur and diversity. Every phase of intellectual effort participated in the great reaction that dates from the closing decades of the eighteenth century; poesy was transformed, philosophy was reconstructed, eloquence assumed a nobler tone, the discovery of Sanskrit opened up vast fields of linguistic enterprise, and placed upon an enduring basis the magnificent science of comparative Philology. One day was as a thousand years in the growth of the human mind. These distinguishing characteristics of the century have powerfully impressed themselves upon its literary productions, and have infused into them a depth of conception, a comprehensiveness, and a degree of originality, far surpassing the most delicately wrought creations of the preceding century. The gorgeous eloquence of Burke, assuming a richer colouring with the flight of declining years, adorned the dialect of oratory with a diversity of phraseological combinations, many of which have passed from the confines of rhetoric, and have enriched the exuberant affluence of the current speech. The sweet strains of Cowper, breathing the spirit of earnest piety, and pervaded by an originality of style and sentiment to which our literature had long been a stranger, clearly announced the dawn of a new era in our own linguistic history. Compared with any of his predecessors, he is what we may call a natural poet. "He broke through conventional forms and usages in a manner more daring than any English poet before him had done, at least since the genius of Pope had bound in its spell the rhythm of English poetry."

The three great revivals in our literature were in the main effected by the civil and religious convulsions of England and of Europe at the time, and at each of these grand awakenings the impulse seems to have been communicated by a foreign literature, which had developed new life and vigour. In the age of Elizabeth, the inspiration was caught from the literature of Italy; during the reign of Queen Anne from that of France; in the present period, from that of Germany.

Our last great period, extending over half a century from the appearance of Cowper and Burns, is without a parallel in our linguistic history, if we except the age of Elizabeth. In comparing the creations of these two periods, we discover, in the poetical productions of the former, greater license, and at the same time greater flexibility, than in those of the latter; but in some essential respects our more recent poetry is justly entitled to the preference. It is not defaced by the conceits of euphuism, and it is generally more symmetrical and consistent. In form and sentiment, it is often strikingly assimilated to the style of our ancient poesy. It constitutes one of the preëminent excellencies of this last great period, that it exhibits the genius and spirit of the creative era, tempered by the gentler graces of the critical age.

In all that pertains to grace of structure, the poetry of the nineteenth century may fairly claim the preference, notwithstanding the numerous passages of incomparable excellence in the dramas of Shakspere. In elaborate execution, harmonious and elegant versification, some of the poets of the earlier part of the nineteenth century have never been surpassed. Cowper, Keats, Shelley, Byron, Scott, Coleridge, Moore, Campbell, Wordsworth, present an array of poetic genius but little lower than the bright cluster that gilded the "glorious reign of great Elizabeth." The exquisite perception of natural loveliness, the rich vocabulary, that distinguish the poetry of Wordsworth; the rare verbal discrimination, Spenserian fancy, and Platonic tenderness, that reign throughout the pages of Coleridge; the dulcet strains of Keats, imbued with the very soul of poesy, established their right of succession, as the lineal heirs of Chaucer, of Shakspere, and Milton. Under the influence of these great masters, the poetic dialect was again enriched by a copious revival of Anglo-Saxon words; the nervous diction of our elder poets and thinkers was called into requisition; familiar and homely phrases were freely admitted into the vocabulary of poetry, which now lost its urban and conventional character; the ancient fountains of the speech were again explored; the process of dialectic regeneration was again vigourously at work, and much of the buried and forgotten wealth of our language was reclaimed; the Elizabethan masters were studied with interest; imitations of their style were not unfrequent, and the merits of Shakspere were at last recognized and appreciated.

By the close of the Georgian era (1830), the poetic spirit seemed to have spent its mightiest energies, and by a transition familiar in the history of every language, the supremacy began gradually to revert to prose, which during the Victorian age has maintained the ascendency. Macaulay and De Quincey attained the same brilliant distinction in prose composition that Shelley, Byron, and Coleridge had won in the domain of poesy, and the present poet laureate is the only worthy representative of that illustrious throng which cast so bright a glow over the closing years of the eighteenth, and the first decades of the nineteenth century. Since the close of the Georgian era there have doubtless been some essential changes in the language, but they will be more distinctly perceptible to succeeding generations than to our own. They do not therefore fall properly within the scope of this history, and must be reserved for future consideration and discussion.

www.ingramcontent.com/pod-product-compliance
Lightning Source LLC
Chambersburg PA
CBHW022014220426
43663CB00007B/1082